UNDERSTANDING
KINGSLEY AMIS

Understanding Contemporary British Literature

Matthew J. Bruccoli, *Editor*

Understanding Graham Greene
by R. H. Miller

Understanding Doris Lessing
by Jean Pickering

Understanding Arnold Wesker
by Robert Wilcher

Understanding Kingsley Amis
by Merritt Moseley

UNDERSTANDING
Kingsley
AMIS

by MERRITT MOSELEY

UNIVERSITY OF SOUTH CAROLINA PRESS

Copyright © 1993 University of South Carolina

Published in Columbia, South Carolina, by the
University of South Carolina Press

Manufactured in the United States of America

Library of Congress Cataloging-in-Publication Data

Moseley, Merritt, 1949–
    Understanding Kingsley Amis / by Merritt Moseley.
      p.   cm.—(Understanding contemporary British literature)
    Includes bibliographical references and index.
    ISBN 0-87249-861-1
    1. Amis, Kingsley—Criticism and interpretation.   I. Title.
II. Series.
PR6001.M6Z79   1993
826'.91409—dc20   92-37274

To

my mother and father

CONTENTS

EDITOR'S PREFACE

Understanding Contemporary British Literature has been planned as a series of guides or companions for students as well as good nonacademic readers. The editor and publisher perceive a need for these volumes because much of the influential contemporary literature makes special demands. Uninitiated readers encounter difficulty in approaching works that depart from the traditional forms and techniques of prose and poetry. Literature relies on conventions, but the conventions keep evolving; new writers form their own conventions—which in time may become familiar. Put simply, *UCBL* provides instruction in how to read certain contemporary writers—identifying and explicating their material, themes, use of language, point of view, structures, symbolism, and responses to experience.

The word *understanding* in the series title was deliberately chosen. Many willing readers lack an adequate understanding of how contemporary literature works; that is, what the author is attempting to express and the means by which it is conveyed. Although the criticism and analysis in the series have been aimed at a level of general accessibility, these introductory volumes are meant to be applied in conjunction with the works they cover. Thus they do not provide a substitute for the works and authors they introduce, but rather prepare the reader for more profitable literary experiences.

M. J. B.

UNDERSTANDING
KINGSLEY AMIS

CHAPTER ONE

Career and Overview

Career

Since 1954, when the publication of *Lucky Jim* put him into the front ranks of "new British writers" (he had published poetry earlier but without any resulting visibility), Kingsley Amis has been one of the most prolific, most widely discussed, most satisfying and most exasperating of novelists writing in English. He has been a social critic of the Left and Right, and he has been described as a proletarian boor and an elitist dandy, both Philistine and University Wit.

Born in 1922 into a lower-middle-class family in South London, he received a good education at the City of London School and, after an interruption for wartime service, earned a B.A. in English (with first-class Honors) in 1947. From 1942 to 1945 he served in the Royal Corps of Signals, ending his war service in Europe and rising to the rank of lieutenant. After taking his B.A., he remained in Oxford to take a B. Litt. degree, but he failed the examination on his B. Litt. thesis.

This failure seemed to have no ill effects on Amis's prospects for university teaching, so, though he had long hoped to make a career as a writer, and had had some of his verse published in *Bright November* (1947), he began his post-Oxford life as an academic. Having married his first wife (Hilary Bardwell) in 1948, and with two children to support, he became a lecturer in English at the University College of Swansea in Wales, remaining in that post from 1949 until 1961. During that period he published his first four novels: *Lucky Jim* (1954), *That Uncertain Feeling* (1955), *I Like It Here* (1958), and *Take a Girl Like You* (1960). He was a visiting fellow in creative writing at Princeton University in 1958–59.

In 1961 Amis was appointed to a fellowship at Peterhouse of Cambridge, where he was generally disappointed with the university and the culture of the place; in 1963 he left academic life and, aside from a short spell at Vanderbilt University in 1967–68, he has been a full-time writer ever since.

His early novels, particularly *Lucky Jim,* led reviewers and commentators to place Amis among the "Angry Young Men," a "school" of writers, largely defined as such by journalists, the supposed character of which was that they were non-upper-class intellectuals who wrote about disaffected provincials who were angry at society. Others often included in the group were John Osborne (whose play *Look Back in Anger* [1956] may have supplied the catch-phrase, while the similarity of names between his Jimmy Porter and Amis's Jim Dixon was probably instrumental in suggesting a connection between Amis and the group); John Wain (author of *Hurry on Down,* 1953); Colin Wilson (*The Outsider,* 1956); Iris Murdoch (*Under the Net,* 1954); and John Braine (*Room at the Top,* 1957). Amis's politics actually were left-wing at this time. He had joined the Communist Party in his youth and he later wrote

CAREER AND OVERVIEW

pamphlets in support of the Fabian Society. Since then, he has gradually and steadily moved rightward.

In his private—or rather public, but non-literary—life, this rightward turn began to appear in his authorship of public statements on the state of English life, and particularly of the so-called Black Papers on education: these were manifestos designed to counter the official government "White Papers" by pointing up a general decline in educational standards. Amis's argument against "democratization" of education— "more will mean worse," particularly when applied to universities—is in fact visible as early as *Lucky Jim*. But he put forth his arguments more forcefully and nonfictionally in the 1960s. He also spoke up against Communism—for instance, opposing the campaign to elect Yevgeny Yevtushenko to the Chair of Poetry at Oxford—and in favor of the U.S. role in Vietnam. The 1960s were, he explains, "the period of the so-called Fascist lunches at Bertorelli's Restaurant in Charlotte Street," a weekly gathering of sympathetically inclined persons ranging from conservative to, it seems, quite seriously Rightist fringe positions.[1] The diners included Robert Conquest, the novelist John Braine, Anthony Powell, and among others Nicholas Ridley, who later became a famous minister for Margaret Thatcher and lost his job in a blaze of bad publicity after intemperate remarks against the Common Market in which he seemed to claim that the Germans were still Nazis. Malcolm Bradbury comments on Amis's political evolution: "Amis's politics moved toward the Right, and today he defines himself as a non-wet [i.e., hard-line] and presumably Thatcherite Tory 'with a few liberal bits,' on hanging, homosexuality, abortion. But the 'liberal bits' are only occasionally noticeable. . . ."[2]

UNDERSTANDING KINGSLEY AMIS

This conservative trend also began to be perceptible in Amis's novels of the 1960s, in which he turned his attention from the unsatisfied outsider figure to insiders who were often portrayed as obnoxious representatives of a somewhat shoddy decade. In 1965 he divorced his first wife and married the novelist Elizabeth Jane Howard. His novels of the 1960s—the "mainstream" books at any rate—feature a closer, perhaps more cynical, look at the morals and follies of marriage, sex, and the relationships between men and women. In these books, it is also no longer possible to think of Amis as just a comic, or humorous, writer. The turn toward deeper seriousness that first appeared in *Take a Girl Like You* (1960) is echoed in the frequent sadness and the wasted emotion and wasted lives of books such as *One Fat Englishman* (1963), *The Anti-Death League* (1966), and *The Green Man* (1969). Notable, too, in this period is his greater interest in experimenting with "genre" fiction—mysteries, ghost stories, science fiction, and James Bond books.

Another trait increasingly perceptible as Amis entered the 1970s was a concern with the effects of aging. Though *Girl, 20* (1971) is about an aging Lothario making a terrible fool of himself over a teenaged girl, *Ending Up* (1973) first squarely addresses such issues as loss of memory, the loneliness of the old, and other unpleasant aspects of aging, while remaining a very funny book.

Though writing novels has always been his primary activity, Amis has also contributed steadily to periodicals, both opinion pieces and hundreds of book reviews; he has edited a dozen books and written introductions to others, continued to

CAREER AND OVERVIEW

write short fiction and poetry (though not very much of either) and written books on drinking, one of his enduring loves.

Amis's son Martin became a precocious writer, a prolific journalist, a literary editor, and the author of six novels so far. That he is something of an experimental writer and an admirer of the high modernists whom Amis despises has drawn some public criticism from the father, but they appear to admire each other in an uncomplicated and uncompetitive way. In 1980 Kingsley Amis and Elizabeth Jane Howard separated, and he moved into an unexpected living arrangement in which he shares lodgings with his first wife and her third husband.

The 1980s saw Amis returning to a very high level of accomplishment, with such novels as *Stanley and the Women* (1984), which created great controversy over its alleged misogyny; *The Old Devils,* (1986); and *Difficulties with Girls* (1988). In 1986 he won the Booker-McConnell Prize, the most prestigious literary award for British and Commonwealth fiction, for *The Old Devils*, and he had been made a Commander of the Order of the British Empire in 1981. In 1990 he published *The Folks That Live on the Hill* and *The Amis Collection: Selected Non-Fiction 1954–1990,* and in that same year he was knighted. In 1991 he brought out his *Memoirs.*

Overview

Ordinarily, *understanding* Kingsley Amis presents no great difficulty. That is to say that his novels seldom require complex exegesis; his language is, though not mathematical or transparent, nevertheless lucid. And this dedication to clarity is an important part of his own program as a writer. He has cast scorn on modern obscurantism and insisted on the writer's obligation to be clear. Asked about experimental prose, he responded, "I can't bear it. I dislike, as I think most readers dislike, being in the slightest doubt about what is taking place, what is meant. I don't want full and literal descriptions of everything, and I'm prepared to take a hint from the author as well as the next man, but I dislike mystification."[3] Amis has no great use for academic literary criticism, either, and his opinion of writers whose books *require* work to be done on them by critics before they can be understood is low.

In another sense, it *is* necessary to make an effort to understand Amis. From the beginning of his career, with the publication of *Lucky Jim* in 1954, he has been condemned to short-sighted or overly narrow reception. *Lucky Jim* is comic; it contains an impatience with "culture" and "the intellectual life" easily attributable to its author; it can be construed as "angry," in the special 1950s sense of that word. All these traits lend themselves to easy generalization and, pretty quickly, to dismissal. And having fixed these traits in their minds, Amis's critics can use them to judge his further writing and living—whether he "remains true" to what they take to be his faith or changes it for something different.[4] That is, if *Lucky Jim* and its immediate successors are taken to be sympathetic studies of the working class, possibly by one of its members, then a later novel about the upper middle classes (*I Want It Now* or *Girl, 20*) can be seen as a betrayal. Likewise,

CAREER AND OVERVIEW

Amis's increasingly conservative stance of the 1960s and 1970s is easy to read as hypocritical or artificial given his well-known leftish beliefs in the 1950s. On the other hand, it is also possible to mark him down for continuing to write the same kind of books or to believe the same ideas, as if changing one's beliefs were inevitable.

All writers are subject to misjudgment, all literary journalists and reviewers—and indeed readers—detect patterns either sustained or fragmented, and there is no need to complain unduly about the treatment of Kingsley Amis in this regard. But there is a need to take a wider view, to look at his career *as* a career and not as a diagram, and to acknowledge how widely, how diversely he has written. It is no shame to say that his accomplishment is uneven. Whose is not?

That accomplishment meets, when viewed as a whole, a very high standard. It has been achieved by a completely serious commitment to an artistic purpose in the face of some discouragements. This may seem an odd claim to make, since far from seeing his commitment to an artistic purpose doom him to penury and oblivion, Amis has published his novels without undue difficulty, made a good living from them— most of his books are still, or at least again, in print—and been rewarded with acclaim including honors by his sovereign. Moreover, the artistic purpose to which he has been committed is the apparently old-fashioned, or middlebrow, one of entertaining readers, amusing them, giving them a plot with interesting characters, and so on. But, though an artistic credo that declares the artist's autonomy and refusal to compromise in the interests of the reader's needs is the kind most modernist writers affirm, Amis's idea of the novelist's role is an artistic one, and not without its own costs.

One reason for some misreading of the Amis canon, by American readers at least, may be the sizable difference between career patterns for established American and British novelists. On average, British novelists seem to be more completely dependent on their writing for their incomes, and (perhaps *therefore*) more prolific and more diverse in their activities. In America the novelist—not to mention the poet—very often draws a salary from a university, either as a faculty member in a writing program or, more undemandingly, as writer in residence. The consequences of this situation are varied. One of them, certainly, is a defense against the necessity of undertaking hack work just for money. Another, presumably, is the ability of more people to *be* novelists than can be supported by books sales alone.

Of the more questionable fruits of the American symbiosis between writers and universities, an unsympathetic commentator (Amis, for instance, or Gore Vidal) might mention the "academic" type of fiction written by authors whose world is academic. The academic placement leads the novelist, it can be argued, to see academia as the audience for his novels.[5] He is not really dependent on the members of the book-buying public for his income, and he thus becomes indifferent to their needs. His books become *recherché*, full of devices that increase their difficulty but provide work for academic study.[6]

And such a novelist no longer writes very much. Removed from market pressures, he spends years in lapidary work over his books before bringing them to the public. Another force for low output, Amis has claimed, is the American desire to write a *great* novel, maybe "*the* great American novel," every time. The results of the academic cushion and gigantic ambitiousness, the unsympathetic critic would argue, are a straining for effect, a removal from the concerns of ordinary readers, and a new novel every ten years. For these and other reasons, Amis argues, "writers and artists in that country seem destined to be or to become stricken deer, misfits, assorted victims and freaks, drunks rather than mere drinkers, hermits, suicides,"[7] and this distaste helps to explain why his stays at Princeton and Vanderbilt were not prolonged or repeated.

The British situation is very different. Though some novelists there are also university teachers—David Lodge and Malcolm Bradbury perhaps the best known—most novelists write for a living. They publish more often than most Americans manage (American prodigies like John Updike and Joyce Carol Oates are the exceptions to the rule). Iris Murdoch, born in 1919, is the author of some thirty-three books; David Lodge, born in 1935, has published fifteen books, most of them while teaching full-time; A. N. Wilson, born in 1950, has published at least sixteen books; Anthony Burgess, a late starter, has written more than thirty novels since 1958 and a profusion of other books of literary criticism, biography, linguistics, travel, and children's literature. Amis, of course, about the same age as Burgess and Murdoch, is the author of thirty books and editor or co-author of a good many others. All these authors are critically respected. No one suggests that they produce hack work.

UNDERSTANDING KINGSLEY AMIS

While presumably no English author decides to publish inferior work, nevertheless the expectation of writing another novel quite soon and thus having another book out in, say, a year and a half or two years is a powerful solvent of the anxiety over the blockbuster from which some Americans seem to suffer. Unless they become international best-sellers, successful British novels sell fewer copies than successful American novels, because of the smaller population and reading public. This fact again militates for greater productivity on the part of the novelist who needs to keep his or her living standard at an acceptable level, and probably helps to explain also why so many British novelists turn up on television and radio frequently, why they review books, write biographies, edit parts of magazines, and otherwise supplement their incomes with literary work. The economics of their situation encourages the ''man of letters'' rather than the austerely dedicated novelist.

In this respect, Amis is a typical English writer. His bibliography includes more novels than anything else, but there is a generous amount of literary and other journalism in *What Became of Jane Austen? and Other Questions* (1970) and *The Amis Collection* (1990). He has written for television and carried out various other projects, such as his book on Kipling and the editing of two recent anthologies of poems, which seem to result from the view that *a writer writes,* coupled (perhaps) with Dr. Johnson's conviction that no man but a blockhead ever wrote for anything except money.

From the beginning of his career, it has been customary to see Amis as like either his contemporaries (John Braine, John Wain, John Osborne) or realistic writers with a social concern

CAREER AND OVERVIEW

like H. G. Wells, Angus Wilson, or C. P. Snow. Malcolm Bradbury insists that the proper comparison is with Evelyn Waugh, and in saying why, he points out Amis's representative quality:

> both . . . turned, with their virtues and their faults, into major writers whose mixture of basic craft, remarkable social perception, comic vision and gift for rage and outrage managed to construct a lifetime of writing of extraordinary dimensions and decided influence. . . . Both suggest that the comic is both a stylistic capacity and a form of human pain, and both indicate what I think is a very British way of dealing with it which may have striking limitations and peculiar strengths.[8]

Finally, Amis is a typical English novelist (of his generation, anyway) in his lack of pomposity about his calling, his ready demystification of the writer's art.

He has spent thirty years deriding the Romantic pose of the artist who is "different" from ordinary people, more sensitive and less accountable to ordinary morality or common sense. The portrayal of Bertrand in *Lucky Jim* satirizes the special claim of the avant-garde, and Amis's writing about Dylan Thomas over the years—both in nonfiction reminiscences and in the fictional portraits of Gareth Probert in *That Uncertain Feeling* and Brydan in *The Old Devils*—suggests that he sees this claim as a self-indulgent affectation. In response to interviewers' questions about his writing, Amis is careful to be offhand about his work. He told Clive James, "In general, you tend to overestimate the part played in a novelist's career by planning, forethought, purpose (and, in the opposite direction, money and fame), while underestimating the role of chance, whim, laziness, excess of energy, boredom, desire to entertain oneself, wanting a change for change's sake. The novelist, of course, *over*estimates the role of these things.''[9] But to compare Amis to Anthony Burgess or Iris Murdoch in terms of working practice or productivity is not to characterize what sort of novelist he is. There are two definitions that both apply: he is a comic novelist, or humorist; and he is a moralist.

In *I Like It Here*, Amis's protagonist pays tribute to Henry Fielding as "the only non-contemporary novelist who could be read with unaffected and whole-hearted interest, the only one who never had to be apologized for or excused on the grounds of changing taste."[10] This endorsement confirms the evidence of the early books as to Amis's aims as a novelist. Fielding was a realist, of a sort, and a comic moralist; he saw the function of humor as regulatory or thermostatic, raising laughter at the character flaws of the people in his books. Amis would not make such extravagant claims for his work as Fielding did for his own, but he does aim to make people laugh, and more than anything else, readers are made to laugh at affectation and hypocrisy. John McDermott calls him "our supreme scourge of cant."[11] In *Lucky Jim*, much of the comedy derives from Jim's sharp awareness of the difference between what people are and what they pretend to be—for instance, between Margaret's image of herself as a jaded and rather dangerous sophisticate and the reality that she is a plain, uninteresting failure—and this distance is often registered in

CAREER AND OVERVIEW

the affectations and distortions of language. Throughout his career, Amis has targeted the pretense of hipness (*Girl, 20*), Welshness (*The Old Devils*), love (*One Fat Englishman*), aging gracefully (*Ending Up*), and, more often than he receives credit for, the pretense of loving women by men who actually hate them (*Jake's Thing, The Green Man*).

There are, of course, other sources of humor in Amis. He is extraordinary in picking out details of speech that can be put to comic effect (Bertrand's "you sam" in *Lucky Jim;* the southern American accent that converts "I'm a gettin pissed off" into "Armageddon pier staff"; the excesses of jargon, particularly academic or psychiatric). Witty descriptions of places and people provide a rich vein of humor, as when a drunken Jim feels that "his face was heavy, as if little bags of sand had been painlessly sewn into various parts of it, dragging the features away from the bones, if he still had bones in his face."[12] And he is good with comic incident—as an admirer of Fielding ought to be—often physical discomfiture involving drinking, sex, or both.

The mistake has sometimes been made of assuming that the author whose works are funny cannot also be serious, or cannot be serious about important things, a kind of *mis*understanding Kingsley Amis that needs rectification. For instance, James Gindin believes that in Amis's novels, "morality is simply material—conversational, controversial at times, but never the issue along which the novel is directed."[13] When Gindin writes that sexual morality is not an important part of *Take a Girl Like You,* it appears that concentration on comedy (his chapter on Amis is called "Kingsley Amis's Funny

Novels'') may have blinded him to the moral dimension of the fiction. Another critic, writing in 1960, prophesied inaccurately that Amis's "failing to treat a serious theme" would "always keep him out of the ranks of significant writers" and blamed this failing on Amis's stylistic success, particularly his use of parody.[14] A more just account of Amis's work comes from Martin Green, who compares him favorably with Shaw and Waugh, explaining that "his humor is much more thoroughly moral than either Shaw's or Waugh's, and with a very different kind of morality: it is essentially concerned with self-questioning and self-criticism, with the difficulties of the sexual life, and with emotional and intellectual sincerity."[15] And Richard J. Voorhees finds, in a comparison which would undoubtedly please Amis, that "if he has something of Fielding's comic skill, he also has Fielding's moral seriousness and simplicity."[16]

Amis has clearly set out to be funny *and* serious, and particularly serious not about politics, or aesthetics, so much as about the moral life of the characters about whom he writes. He speaks in an interview of the importance of making his bad characters ridiculous: "In my novels there are good people and bad people, which is very rare these days. There's often a lot wrong with the good people, and one must also lay off by making the bad people say good things or be right about things that the good people are wrong about. There are bad people, and it is essential to make them ridiculous."[17] If Amis has sometimes failed to make his concern with goodness clear to readers, there are several reasons (in addition to people's fixed convictions that funny things are about something less than good and evil). One of these arises from his abilities as a "mimic," which permit him to inhabit his characters; most of his novels have a detached point of view but long passages of indirect free style, where the narrating voice is using the language and attitudes of the character. Brigid Brophy complains that the author "consistently ignores the elementary requirement that a storyteller should distinguish between straight narrative and reporting of the character's consciousness" so that "we cannot tell whether Mr. Amis shares his heroes' morality. . . . "[18] This is an odd complaint against a practice so common in modern literature (the stock technique of Virginia Woolf, for instance). Edmund Wilson, writing about *That Uncertain Feeling,* recognizes the difficulty but advises discriminating reading: "We see only so much of the world as he [John Lewis, the protagonist] knows, and this seems to make it hard for some readers to correct the illusions and distortions of his limited point of view, and to lead them more easily to attribute the reaction of the character to the author, to suppose that the author is not aware of how disgusting his protagonist's life is and of how badly he and his friends are behaving."[19]

Most of Amis's novels explore important ethical questions, perhaps most memorably the morality of sexual exploitation by one person of another, but also the ethical imperialism of the rich, seduction and infidelity, parental responsibility for a mad son, and treachery against nation or friend. But the way to continue the specific consideration of these points is by looking at the novels themselves.

Notes

1. Kingsley Amis, *Memoirs* (New York: Summit Books, 1991) 147.

2. Malcolm Bradbury, *No, Not Bloomsbury* (New York: Columbia University Press, 1988) 205.

3. Michael Barber, "The Art of Fiction LIX: Kingsley Amis," *Paris Review* 64 (1975): 47.

4. Leslie Paul, in "The Angry Young Men Revisited," *Kenyon Review* 27 (Spring 1965), takes the approach of finding Amis wanting in fidelity to what Paul thinks is his real subject and attitude.

5. Peter Firchow, ed., "Kingsley Amis," in *The Writer's Place: Interviews on the Literary Situation in Contemporary Britain* (Minneapolis: University of Minnesota Press, 1974) 22: Amis criticizes "novels that seem to get written for an audience of academics," written "to appeal to campus classes and discussion groups.

6. See Gore Vidal, *At Home: Essays 1982–1988* (New York: Vintage Books, 1990) 179–80: today's typical novelist, "in the summers and on sabbatical, . . . will write novels that others like himself will want to teach just as he, obligingly, teaches their novels . . . What tends to be left out of these works is the world. World gone, no voluntary readers."

7. Amis, *Memoirs* 201.

8. Bradbury 206.

9. Clive James, "Profile 4: Kingsley Amis," *The New Review* 1 (July 1974): 28.

10. Kingsley Amis, *I Like It Here* (New York: Harcourt, Brace, 1958) 185. Compare Amis's remarks to Barber 49.

11. John McDermott, *Kingsley Amis: An English Moralist* (New York: St. Martin's, 1989) 33.

12. Kingsley Amis, *Lucky Jim* (Garden City, NY: Doubleday, 1954) 62.

13. James Gindin, *Postwar British Fiction: New Accents and Attitudes* (Berkeley: University of California Press, 1962) 41.

14. Peter Hilty, "Kingsley Amis and Mid-Century Humor," *Discourse* 3 (January 1960): 44.

15. Martin Green, "British Comedy & The British Sense of Humour: Shaw, Waugh, and Amis," *Texas Quarterly* 4 (Autumn 1961): 225–26; cf. George Watson's claim that "the new English novel" of the 1950s, notably *Amis's* fiction, "is about the search for goodness. . . . " "The Coronation of Realism," *The Georgia Review* 41 (Spring 1987): 13.

CAREER AND OVERVIEW

16. Richard J. Voorhees, "Kingsley Amis: Three Hurrahs and a Reservation," *Queens Quarterly* 74 (Spring 1972): 46.

17. Dale Salwak, "An Interview with Kingsley Amis," *Contemporary Literature* 16 (1975): 5.

18. Brigid Brophy, *Don't Never Forget* (New York: Holt, Rinehart & Winston, 1966) 218–19.

19. Edmund Wilson, *The Bit Between My Teeth: A Literary Chronicle of 1950–1965* (New York: Farrar, Straus and Giroux, 1965) 278.

CHAPTER TWO

Amis's Novels in the 1950s

Lucky Jim (1954)

. . . nice things are nicer than nasty ones.

Kingsley Amis's career has extended now for over thirty-five years, and he is not just visible as a former novelist still lingering among us, but as a vital writer publishing good novels and winning new critical esteem. Nevertheless, there is a sense in which he is a man of the 1950s. For one thing, some of the values of the fiction he has written in the 1980s and 1990s are redolent of attitudes more associated with those postwar years—for instance, the attitude toward women, uncomplicated notions of equality, which many of his characters hold, or the anti-Communism that still fixes on the Soviet invasion of Hungary in 1956. For another, as he writes often about people his own age, his characters often have a sympathetic or psychological link to the 1950s when they were young.

But the most important reason for this identification is that Amis's first novel, *Lucky Jim,* is one of the key books of

AMIS'S NOVELS IN THE 1950s

the English 1950s. To begin with the most important point, it is one of the best. But it also illustrates much that is significant in 1950s fiction, and as an example or clarion, it helped to change the face of English writing. Malcolm Bradbury writes that this "became a summative work of the new spirit in fiction much as John Osborne's *Look Back in Anger* did in drama," and that, mostly because of *Lucky Jim,* Amis's "impact on the 1950s came to rival that of Waugh on the 1920s."[1] Many other tributes show its liberating effect, which had two parts. One was the way in which it was written; the other, its subject matter and particularly the kind of hero it featured.

Rubin Rabinovitz, in *The Reaction Against Experiment in the English Novel, 1950–1960,* surveys a group of novelists who rebelled against modernism in prose fiction on various grounds including its obscurity, detachment from the concerns of everyday life, preciousness, foreignness, and alleged indifference to plot and character. Rabinovitz identifies the leaders in "a return to traditional forms" as C. P. Snow, Angus Wilson, and Amis.[2] Of these Amis is clearly the "younger generation" representative. James Gindin lists their characteristics as "their formal conservatism and their attempts to revive older novelistic traditions, their insistence on man's limitations, their comic perspective, and their partial or hesitant commitment"—which he suggests are eighteenth-century qualities.[3]

There is no question that, as his acerbic comments show, Amis is hostile to what is usually thought of as experimental fiction (though he also objects to "the experimental" being limited to certain types of experimentation and not others, such as new subjects). But *Lucky Jim* is much more than a backlash: it is something new. David Lodge, whose admiration for high modernist writing is unmistakable, also acknowledges the liberating effect of this novel:

> *Lucky Jim* (1954), a book of great verbal dexterity disguising itself as clumsiness, but rooted in an English tradition of comedy of manners quite foreign to Joyce. *Lucky Jim* was another magic book for me—and for most English readers of my age and background, upwardly mobile, scholarship-winning, first-generation university graduates—for it established precisely the linguistic register we needed to articulate our sense of social identity, a precarious balance of independence and self-doubt, irony and hope.[4]

Those for whom the significance of *Lucky Jim* lay in its new kind of hero include Walter Allen, who writes that Jim Dixon was "a symbol . . . a figure to be identified with . . . an archetypal figure, the hero of a generation in the everlasting battle between the generations."[5] Those who identified with Jim clearly found something refreshing in his irreverence, his powerlessness, his comic (though bloodless) rebellion against the forces of "the Establishment," which disgusted him and frustrated his desire to have nice things. Another key to the reader's identification would have been that Jim is really not a hero. Neither is he an anti-hero of the Underground Man sort; he is a non-hero; that is, an ordinary man with ordinary desires and ordinary reactions to his experience. Though Jim (unlike most people in Britain then, as now) is a teacher at a university, he is by no means an intellectual. Unsure of the history which he is paid to teach but in which he can hardly be bothered to appear interested, his relationship to the university is that of anxious job-seeker to employer. His real interests are in companionship with unaffected, interesting male friends, in enjoying drinking and smoking, in preserving a decent life on a small salary, and in women. Martin Green allies Amis rather oddly with D. H. Lawrence and F. R. Leavis, the influential Cambridge don, Lawrence-admirer, and spokesman for the "Great Tradition," who once denounced Amis, in his Cambridge years, as a pornographer; but he acutely identifies "Amis's image of the lower middle class, non-gentlemanly conscience, the creation of which is his great achievement."[6]

In fact, Jim is aggressively hostile to many aspects of "culture," as seen most famously in his reference to "filthy Mozart!" and his pretense to be ignorant of cultural facts he really knows. Many reviewers, and critics writing retrospectively, have made the mistake of identifying Jim's Philistinism as Amis's: one critic, commenting on Jim's phrase "filthy Mozart!" suggests that *Amis* "is too obviously cultured to hate culture that much; one suspects his sincerity"; and another huffs: "It is no use saying that Lucky Jim dramatized opinions that Amis did not necessarily hold himself. Amis, in his treatment of what Somerset Maugham called, with some irritation, 'the white collar proletariat,' *was* Lucky Jim. . . . "[7] Understanding Amis requires that readers not rush to identify opinions expressed by his characters with his own, to attribute Jim's attitude to culture to his creator; but it

is probably wrong even to attribute it to Jim. In the company
of pretentious art-sniffers and poseurs whom he hates, he is
driven in the opposite direction, toward a lowbrow rejection of
high art, as a way of rejecting *them*. Very likely the attitudes
expressed by Jim towards medieval art and modern art ("the
work of some kindergarten oaf") are in fact those of the author—that is, values the novel upholds—but the rejection of
Mozart and part-singing are the reactions of an ordinary man
stung by pomposity—the pomposity of the music-lovers, not
the music. Jim measures their pomposity in his role as "a ba-
rometer of hot air."[8]

    Lucky Jim is a satire, and in part it is a satire of the ac-
ademic milieu in which Kingsley Amis made his life at the
time of publication. He explains how he came to write the
book (and perhaps why it was dedicated to Philip Larkin):
he was visiting Larkin at Leicester University in 1948. "On
the Saturday morning he had to go into college and took me
("hope you won't mind—they're all right really") to the common room for a quick coffee. I looked round a couple of times
and said to myself, 'Christ, somebody ought to do something
with this.' Not that it was awful—well, only a bit; it was
strong and sort of *developed*, a whole mode of existence no
one had got on to from outside, like the SS in 1940, say."[9]

    But the book is more than a satire: it is a comic romance.
In some ways, Jim reenacts the Cinderella myth. He is unjustly doomed to low status and to enduring his own servility
towards unworthy and even evil people. He must truckle toward Professor Welch, attend his deadly parties, do his library
research for him, in hopes of retaining a job that is not what he

wants anyway. Moreover, he has become trapped in a relationship with Margaret Peel, a somewhat shrewish and certainly
manipulative colleague—trapped in part by Margaret's manipulations, including a suicide attempt, and partly by his own
feelings that "the huge class that contained Margaret was destined to provide his own womenfolk: those in whom the in-
tention of being attractive could sometimes be made to get
itself confused with performance; those with whom a too-tight
skirt, a wrong-coloured, or no, lipstick, even an ill-executed
smile could instantly discredit that illusion beyond apparent
hope of renewal."[10] Jim's twin predicaments—what to do
about Margaret and how to secure his job with Professor
Welch—are both illustrations of the "idea of good things going wrong or being got wrong," and they occupy much of the
novel and give it both its tension and much of its comedy.[11]
The complicating factor is the introduction of Bertrand, the
obnoxious son of Professor Welch, along with his beautiful
girl, Christine Callaghan. Almost against his will, and certainly with no conviction that it can make a difference to his
predestined linkage with Margaret, Jim begins to take an interest in Christine; surprisingly, she responds; he discovers
that the unpleasant qualities he had seen in her are either sour-
grapes inventions of his own or humanizing traits. Christine is
both beautiful and normal, a combination for which he has no
preparation. But to court Christine entangles him further with
the Welches and puts him at odds with Bertrand and threatens
his relationship with Margaret.

Cinderella wins her prince and dramatic elevation in status when her disguise is penetrated. Much the same happens

with Jim. Throughout the novel, he responds to his position of subservience and even hypocrisy by a variety of funny releases, including telling himself the truths he must suppress for others, making faces and indulging in violent fantasies. For instance, Christine Callaghan says something unwelcome to Jim "in a tone that made him turn his back for a moment at the sideboard and make his Chinese mandarin's face, hunching his shoulders a little" (71). He has recourse elsewhere to his Edith Sitwell face, his sex-life-in-Ancient Rome face, his drunken Eskimo face, and others. As for violent fantasies, Jim, annoyed by the vagaries of Professor Welch, "pretended to himself that he'd pick up his professor round the waist, squeeze the furry grey-blue waistcoat against him to expel the breath, run heavily with him up the steps, along the corridor to the Staff Cloakroom, and plunge the too-small feet in their capless shoes into a lavatory basin, pulling the plug once, twice, and again, stuffing the mouth with toilet-paper" (11–12). And when Margaret produces another emotional crisis designed to put Jim in the wrong, the narrator recounts, "Dixon wanted to rush at her and tip her backwards in the chair, to make a deafening rude noise in her face, to push a bead up her nose. 'How do you mean?' he asked" (161).

This repression, no matter how colorfully relieved, cannot help being painful to Dixon. The moment his life changes, as David Lodge has clearly noted, is when he reunites his thoughts with his actions and speech: "the issues of the novel can only be resolved when Jim wills his inner life to coincide with his outer life."[12] This happens when Jim fights Bertrand and knocks him down and finally says what he thinks: "It was

AMIS'S NOVELS IN THE 1950s

clear that Dixon had won this round, and, it then seemed, the whole Bertrand match. He put his glasses on again, feeling good; Bertrand caught his eye with a look of embarrassed recognition. The bloody old towser-faced boot-faced totem-pole on a crap reservation, Dixon thought. 'You bloody old towser-faced boot-faced totem-pole on a crap reservation,' he said'' (214).

From this point the obstacles to Jim's good fortune are rapidly cleared away. His long-feared public address on ''Merrie England'' is destroyed by his drunkenness, which leads him to say what he really thinks about the Middle Ages, rather than what Professor Welch wants him to say. A discussion with Margaret Peel's former beau relieves him of the guilt feelings which have bound Jim to her. Liberated from Margaret, he is free to pursue, and win, Christine; liberated from Professor Welch (by having been fired), he is free to be given a much better job, working in London for Christine's uncle, the wealthy Julius Gore-Urquhart, as a ''boredom-detector'' (219). He really has been lucky. The novel ends with a great purgative blast of laughter at the Welches.

The satisfactions of *Lucky Jim* include the sharp satire on all that is both worthless and pretentious about academic life; the shapely plot and the careful way it rewards ordinary virtue (Jim's) with conventional goods (improved fortune, the love of a beautiful woman); and the rich comedy. *Lucky Jim* is one of the funniest of all twentieth-century novels. The humor lies partly in farcical situations like Jim's drunken destruction of his bedclothes and his desperate attempts the following morning to hide the evidence, or his disastrous Merrie England lecture. An even larger contribution is made by the language. Malcolm Bradbury writes that in *Lucky Jim* Amis's language "was able to construct a sceptical social and moral realism which found sense, dismissed aesthetic over-formulation, knocked against pretension, and gave to the stuff of ordinary life a comic enjoyment, a reinvigoration of the banal."[13] The book is rich in observations like the description of Professor Welch as looking like "an African savage being shown a simple conjuring trick" (14) or on another occasion "canted over in his chair like a broken robot" (80). Much of Jim Dixon's passion goes into his fear and contempt of Welch, so it is not surprising that he finds funny ways of scorning Welch. One way is Jim's "Welch tune":

> This tune featured in the "rondo" of some boring piano concerto Welch had once insisted on playing him. . . . Dixon had fitted words to it. Going down the stairs towards the Common Room, where coffee would be available, he articulated these words behind closed lips: "You *ig*norant clod, you *stu*pid old sod, you *ha*vering *sla*vering get . . ." Here intervened a string of unmentionables, corresponding with an oom-pah sort of effect in the orchestra. "You *wo*rdy old *tu*rdy old scum, you *gri*ping old *pi*ping old bum. . . . "(89)

The unsatisfiable aggression of the Welch song is exemplary, and its normality, its appropriateness to the sort of person Jim Dixon is, is also finely adjusted. Jim is an ordinary person (though more interesting to read about than the *average* person would be) and *Lucky Jim* shows at least two important things happening to him: one is that his luck changes so that, from having to subject himself to inferior souls, he is enabled by change of fortune to triumph over them. This is the Cinderella, or romance, plot. The other is that he successfully resists a challenge to his integrity. He is tempted to sell out, to marry Margaret, to be Welch's toady, and for a while he is too weak to resist; but by and by he finds the strength to assert himself against the forces of artifice.

This assertion of his own decency, a moral choice, might in a different novel lead to a darker ending. If it had meant no more than losing his job and Margaret, with no compensating gains, Jim would have been left nobler but more miserable. *Lucky Jim* is a comedy because Jim's unusually good luck coincides with his taking a moral stand. In Amis's novels after *Lucky Jim*, the emphasis will more often fall on the moral stand than on the luck.

That Uncertain Feeling (1955)

Amis's second book, *That Uncertain Feeling*, has several traits familiar to readers of *Lucky Jim*. One of these is its humor, which for various reasons is not so striking as in the earlier novel, but is an important feature both in the satire (some very funny burlesque of the Dylan Thomas school of Welshness), plot developments (for instance, when the narrator finds it necessary to dress in Welsh peasant-woman costume to escape a house party, then must climb down the walls, make his way home on a crowded bus, and so on), and most of all the

UNDERSTANDING KINGSLEY AMIS

vivid language. The narration startles with perfect phrases: there is the chief Welsh phony, Gareth Probert, with his "grub-shaped eyelids," who "sounded like an actor pretending, with fair success on the whole, to be Owain Glyndwr in a play on the Welsh Children's Hour."[14] Elizabeth Gruffydd-Williams and her companion are each characterized in one passage, where "she was wearing an orange-reddish dress which gave her an air of ignorant wildness and freedom, like the drunken daughter of some man of learning," and the companion "met her eye for a moment and then looked suddenly away as if hearing his name called from a secret panel over the fireplace" (30–31).

The protagonist of *That Uncertain Feeling*, John Lewis, is an ordinary sort of man, from a modest background (this time, explicitly working class: his father is a coal miner). He is constrained by circumstances. A librarian, he has no interest in his work; though educated, he prefers to read subliterary material and pretends to be more ignorant than he is. Lewis has a wife and two children, and they live in a poor flat on a very limited (and limiting) income.

The plot represents two challenges to Lewis's integrity, one professional and one sexual. In this, it recalls the Welch and Margaret predicaments Jim Dixon faces, but the resolution will be much messier. One of these challenges is an opening for a new sub-librarian in his library, a promotion with a pay raise which the Lewises badly need. The other is his growing entanglement with a woman called Elizabeth Gruffydd-Williams. Mrs. Gruffydd-Williams, a member of the "Anglicized upper classes" (10), takes a somewhat inexplicable interest in Lewis; or an interest explicable by saying that adulterous relations are among the amusements of the rich, somewhat decadent social circle she moves in, and Lewis is young, attractive enough, and available because he is weak.

John Lewis thinks of himself as hating everything the Gruffydd-Williamses stand for. At their party, he vows that "as a sworn foe of the *bourgeoisie,* and especially the Aberdarcy *bourgeoisie,* I'd see to it that I never came here again" (37). The reason for the vow is not that he finds these particular members of the *bourgeoisie* so repulsive, but that he finds them—or at least Elizabeth—attractive. Naturally, he does not keep to his vow; his next line of defence is that if he can't keep away from them, at least he doesn't have to compromise his principles for them, and soon he is wondering, "Should I break in in a renewed effort to be marked down as 'impossible,' bawl a defence of the Welfare State, start undressing myself or the dentist's mistress, give the dentist a lovely piggy-back round the room, call for a toast to the North Korean Foreign Minister or Comrade Malenkov?" (43). Of course he does none of these things.

Like Jim Dixon, in fact, John Lewis rebels internally, thinking how hateful are the people with whom he continues to associate. (He is the narrator of *That Uncertain Feeling,* and so the reader is given his thoughts, and the contrast between them and his actions, directly).

The promotion to sub-librarian might seem an unalloyed good thing, except for two complications. One is that John Lewis really doesn't care for the librarian's profession, and he finds himself in competition with a colleague, Ieuan Jenkins, who does care for the profession and who is more deserving. Much *more* complicating is the moral contamination of the library question by the Elizabeth question; her husband is an influential member of the library board who can presumably arrange for Lewis to receive the promotion. How should this affect Lewis's relations with Elizabeth? Should he go on *having* any relations with Elizabeth? If so, why?

The novel essentially turns on this moral dilemma, which is primarily about sexual fidelity but also about professional integrity and class. John Lewis is held by the Gruffydd-Williams circle, continues to frequent it, and finally becomes Elizabeth's lover, knowing all the while that he is doing an ignoble thing, and feeling his injustice to his wife Jean. While continuing to despise what the Gruffydd-Williamses stand for, he is able to enjoy it; while never really *liking* Elizabeth, much less approving of her, he is still drawn to her in a crudely baffled way. "It wasn't just that women were a thing that had made a profound impression on me; no, also to be taken into account was the fact that I found women attractive, especially attractive women. Now how had that come about? . . . Why did I like women's breasts so much? I was clear on why I liked them, thanks, but why did I like them *so much*?" (56). Lewis never really doubts that it is wrong to sleep with Elizabeth, though he tries out little justifications on himself. But is it right to take the results of his infidelity—the job rigged for him by Elizabeth's husband—especially after he learns that the main reason he got it was not to please him but to frustrate someone else? He decides, in making a clean breast to Jean, that renouncing Elizabeth includes renouncing the job she procured for him, and he is surprised to find that his wife sees this as a further act of selfishness, as striking a moral posture at the expense of his family, which needs the extra income he is giving up.

The ending of this book and its resolution of the moral questions it raises are much more ambiguous than the ending of *Lucky Jim,* in which regained integrity coincides happily with winning the girl and getting the better, non-compromising job. Here John's gaining the job, though for the wrong reasons and through illicit influence, gives him the raise in pay he really needs, but makes him unhappy and guilty; renouncing it makes him feel virtuous but repels his wife, who has been hurt enough by his infidelity to care only for the increased comfort. He cannot satisfy all his needs and desires together, and perhaps cannot satisfy them at all.

Jim Dixon's credo has been that "nice things are nicer than nasty ones," and luckily he rises above the nasty ones and wins the nice ones. John Lewis has a similarly simple thought: "It wasn't so much doing what you wanted to do that was important, I ruminated, as wanting to do what you did. What about writing that down?" (89) Neither of these is offered as a very complex moral theory or action plan, and John's in particular is clearly useful mostly for self-justification.

Moreover, it fails him. Though he doesn't stop himself from going to the parties of the Anglicized Aberdarcy bourgeoisie, and becoming the lover of one of them, he doesn't succeed, either, in making himself want to do these things. The conclusion of the book, in which the Lewises move to a smaller town and he finds work selling coal, does not cleanly resolve the issues it has raised. The explanation of the dénouement is couched in terms of rediscovered integrity and a farewell to pretension and artifice: "I thought of that upper-class crowd. Why couldn't they be Welsh, I wondered, or since they were mostly Welsh by birth, why couldn't they stay Welsh? Why had they got to go around pretending to be English all the time?—not that there was anything, or anything very serious, wrong with being English, providing you were it to start with" (232–33).

The application of this line of reasoning to his own condition, and particularly to what he has now decided is the crucial end of saving his marriage, leads him to think: "Since I seemed to have piloted myself into the position of being immoral and moral at the same time, the thing was to keep trying not to be immoral, and then to keep trying might turn into a habit. I was always, at least until I reached the climacteric, going to get pulled two ways, and keeping the pull from going the wrong way, or trying to, would have to take the place, for me, of stability and consistency. Not giving up was the important thing" (233). The contrast between this program of action and his earlier plan, to be happy by contriving to like what you can't help doing, is dramatic.

The final chapter shows a chastened John Lewis back in his home town (clearly a backwater), where the challenges to him from sex and status seem to be starting up again on a lower level and he is resisting them. Clearly, he and Jean are reconciled. It is hard to know whether to read this conclusion as a retreat from temptation, a saving of the soul by running away from the things he knows he can't resist, or a real moral step upward; the second possibility seems overly sentimental for Amis, not ordinarily much given to romantic idealization of small-town life or the nobility of the poor, particularly the Welsh poor. Clearly Jean (like many another woman in Amis's fiction) is a moral norm of some sort, and returning to her, ceasing to hurt her, has to be the right thing for John to do. But the conditions which he seems to believe he must accept in order to do so suggest that real maturity has been deferred, not accepted. "That Uncertain Feeling" refers to the feeling of being in love, but it may also describe the reader's reaction when the book is finished.

I Like It Here (1958)

Amis's next novel, *I Like It Here,* is one which seems to embarrass him (he has called it "a very slipshod, lopsided piece of work"), and though readers need not accept his own ranking of his novels, there is some reason for him to slight this book.[15] Critics have produced extraordinarily mixed reactions to this work, ranging from contemptuous dismissal ("a mishmash"; "barely worth serious consideration, since his careless writing and ambivalent attitude towards the central character almost negate the more praiseworthy features"[16]) to praising the book for something it almost surely is not: "a self-self-parody, a fictional exercise both done and not done *in propria persona,* a parody of an Amis novel as if written by some imitator wishing to try to pass it off as the genuine article": "a satire in the guise of the novel on F. R. Leavis's *The*

Great Tradition.''[17] It repeats some of the same gestures and situations seen in the first two books, but with a lower degree of amusement or subtlety. As in *Lucky Jim*, there is a protagonist who is something of an imposter, whose self-esteem is damaged by his absorption into a role he cannot respect; as in *That Uncertain Feeling*, this man faces moral challenges and resolves them in not wholly satisfactory ways.

One of the features present in the first two books but brought to great prominence here is the philistinism, real or pretended, of the protagonist. As Jim Dixon reflected on ''filthy Mozart'' and John Lewis, though a librarian, thinks of himself as having ''been led by what must have been exceptional boredom to look into a book about Dr. Johnson, of all people'' (37), Garnet Bowen thinks of the surprise in store if ''the *Iliad* or some other gruelling cultural monument had turned out to be a good read as well as a masterpiece''[18] and thinks contemptuously of his student days when he was ''attending a course of lectures on some piece of orang-utan's toilet-requisite from the dawn of England's literary heritage— *The Dream of the Rood*, perhaps, or *The Fall of the Angels*'' (93). The study of educated and cultured people who sneer at education and culture is most clearly presented in this book, in fact, as a sort of self-hatred, based on a knowledge that the philistine is himself in some false position. Jim Dixon is a university lecturer, John Lewis a librarian, Garnet Bowen a writer and lecturer; all find it comforting to pretend to know about literature and art no more than is necessary for making fun of it. Bowen gives himself away accidentally when someone refers to the damaging effects on an artist's career of hostile criticism:

AMIS'S NOVELS IN THE 1950s

"Very much the same sort of thing happened in Elgar's career," Bowen blurted out before he could stop himself. He
tried to cheapen it with "So a fellow was telling me, anyway," but only succeeded in making himself sound modest.
A moral failure on this scale came about through attending
too closely to what people were saying. Those perishing
vodka martinis at the International Musicians' Club that
time must have weakened his protective shell without him
noticing. He had thought that the film-composer chap who
was buying them all had merely been boring him. And now
here was this gross betrayal into non-ironical cultural
discussion. (159)

Added to the usual veneer of disdain for "culture" is Garnet
Bowen's dislike of "abroad." The spring of the book is in the
events which get Bowen, who "likes it here" (i.e., wants to
remain in England,) over to Portugal. There are obvious pre-
tentiousnesses about travel abroad which are accurately skew-
ered in this book, but beyond that is the protective shell again:

Bowen told himself that he suffered from acute prejudice
about abroad. Some of this he thought he recognized as un-
reasonable, based as it was on disinclination for change,
dislike of fixing up complicated arrangements, and fear of
making a fool of himself. . . . Further, he fancied that he
had a long history of lower-middle-class envy directed
against the upper-middle-class traveller who handled foreign railway-officials with insolent ease, discussed the
political situation in fluent *argot,* and landed up first go
at exactly the right hotel, if indeed he wasn't staying

with some *contessa*, all cigarette-holder and *chaise-longue*, who called him by some foreign version of his christian name. (23)

To this fairly clear-sighted account of why Bowen fears "abroad" might be added laziness, a puritanical fear of letting himself go under foreign influences, and "the fact, sadly neglected of recent years, that foreigners talked funny" (46–47). The humor inherent in foreigners talking English or, worse yet, completely foreign languages, is thoroughly explored in this book.

Bowen's exaggeratedly low-brow and isolationist postures seem to derive from self-hatred, and he is quite clear-sighted about his own impostures: "Until a couple of years ago Bowen had been supposed to be a novelist who was keeping himself and his family going on the proceeds of journalism, wireless talks and a bit of lecturing. In the last six months or so he had started being supposed to be a dramatist who was keeping himself and his family going by the same means" (6). As in the conversation about Elgar, he traps himself in an unguarded moment; having pretended to have an idea about a new way of writing about travel, he is surprised to be offered a large advance which effectively traps him into going to Portugal. Then his publisher asks him to investigate the claims of an Englishman residing in Portugal to be the distinguished writer Wulfstan Strether, long silent and thought to be dead. Strether's publisher needs advice on whether "Strether" is who he claims to be, so as to publish his novel without embarrassment from an imposter, and the suggested reward for Bowen's job of "sham-detecting" is a job in the publishing house.

The sham-detecting becomes quite complicated. Bowen is, in part, detecting whether his own posture towards "abroad" is a sham: he must test whether in fact he hates it as much as he has enjoyed claiming he does. He must find out whether the pseudo-Strether is a sham, and in fact he finally decides that the claimant is *such* a pretentious poseur—claiming superiority to Henry Fielding, for instance—that he must be the *authentic* Strether. "Strether" is too much of a sham to be a sham. Finally Bowen must examine the affectation of his own life. He has acknowledged that he is less a real writer than "a man who was supposed to be a writer" (146). His honesty consists in recognizing that he is an imposter; a greater honesty, of course, would require that he stop being one.

Through an undramatic process that includes his encounters with Strether and with Portugal, he seems to make this change. This at least is one interpretation of his determination expressed on his return to England: "But he was going to write something else instead, about a man who was forced by circumstances to do the very thing he most disliked the thought of doing and found afterwards that he was exactly the same man as he was before. Nobody, nobody at all, was going to hear anything about it until it was finished" (207).

I Like It Here is a sort of transitional novel. David Lodge has written admiringly of it as an example of "a special genre . . . the kind of novel which is not so much turned outwards upon the world as inward upon literary art and upon the literary artist himself," and relates it to Waugh's *The Ordeal of Gilbert Pinfold* and Nabokov's *Pale Fire*.[19] Its protagonist, Garnet Bowen, shares with the earlier Jim Dixon and John

UNDERSTANDING KINGSLEY AMIS

Lewis the comic opposition to nasty things, though here its expression has shrunk from inspired face-making to ritual invocation of the word "bum," a vulgar, somewhat childish synonym for "bottom." The ambiguous resolution of the moral issues (though they are not momentous ones) looks toward *Take a Girl Like You* and most of the best of Amis's mature fiction.

Take a Girl Like You (1960)

Take a Girl Like You opened the new decade of the 1960s for Amis, but in many ways it sums up the 1950s. It also has several features that are new. One is that this is not primarily a comic novel. It has many funny things in it, including some sharp satire and some good comedy based on people's dialects and idiolects, but the overall tone is not comic; and the plot has a non-comic movement and resolution. Another is that it is clearly a *bigger* undertaking, more ambitious, broader in scope. There is a main plot, a fairly simple one: man pursues woman, who is attracted to him but wants to put off going to bed with him; eventually he wins; she accepts this resolution, somewhat wistfully. But there are minor lines of development, beyond the perturbations which separate Jenny and Patrick and draw them together again.

There is a more serious attempt at drawing social distinctions based on time and geography, well beyond the kind of Englishman-in-Portugal, or real-Welshman-among-the-phony-

AMIS'S NOVELS IN THE 1950s

Welshmen, contrasts that Amis has used before. This book pivots on a contrast between the industrial North of England, here figuring as more traditional, more stuck in the 1940s, when the south has moved into the 1960s, and its setting in the modern south, particularly the London suburbs, with hedonism, sports cars, pink gin, and a relaxed attitude toward sex. (One recent essay on Amis illustrates the difficulty some readers have in noticing when he stops doing one thing and starts doing another: Terry Teachout writes that this book, "like its predecessors, is set in Amisland, the sooty, shabby industrial town up the road from Wigan Pier. . . . "[20]) The two main characters are examplars of these two societies: Jenny Bunn, a northern girl with strong principles, and Patrick Standish, a southern playboy.

Finally, this novel stands out from those that have gone before in calling forth a strong moral critique of the behavior of its characters, who are judged not just by their failures to be what they seem (though this kind of judgment is there, too), but also by reference to ideas of dignity, kindness, and respect for the autonomy of others.

The social tragicomedy is very carefully done, making itself felt through Patrick Standish and Jenny Bunn. Patrick is a southerner, an educated man (he teaches Latin in a fee-paying school), a sophisticate; he is a drinker, a good-looking seducer, a witty man whose principles—for he has some serious principles—are never quite strong enough to override his desire to do just what he wants to do. As John McDermott says, "In Patrick, charm and goodness have come adrift from each other."[21] Though not wealthy, he lives a life of apparent affluence. And Amis seems to present him as something of the representative figure of the society he inhabits.

His opposite number, sometime girlfriend, and eventual conquest, Jenny Bunn, is a more serious person. She is devoted to her family, though she has left them to come south. Also a teacher (she works in a state-run primary school), she thinks of herself as "the steady type who got married and had babies."[22] Though opposed to premarital sex (this is the key assumption on which the plot turns), she is not a prude exactly, nor cloyingly good. She is attracted to good-looking men like Patrick and experiences sexual desire, but believes waiting until marriage is the right course. On lesser men she can be scathing, ranking various acquaintances as "duds" and "stooges," whom she tries to like but cannot. A nice touch is that Jenny is not pious; though Patrick sneers at her ideas as coming from the Bible class, she holds them without any sanction of religious belief—which makes her lonelier and more vulnerable than if she thought going to bed with Patrick would make her go to Hell. Another complicating factor for Jenny is that she is not only beautiful, but somehow "looks as if" she is sexually experienced and eager.

The contrast between Jenny and Patrick—and by extension the mores he embodies—is nicely summed up when, on an early date with Patrick, she stops his roving hands and goes to make a cup of tea: "She did not want any more chat, but could not think how to say so without running the risk of sounding both stagey and toffee-nosed, without falling into the style of *I don't wish to discuss it further* or even *I'll thank you to take your hands off me* (next stage) in a world of *Ah, come on, relax will you?* and *You don't know what you do to me when you do that*" (60).

Surrounding Patrick and Jenny are a large cast of thoroughly developed secondary characters. Some of them are primarily comic creations, though that is never all they are: in this category are the other inhabitants of Jenny's house, Dick Thompson, the landlord, famous for stinginess; his wife Martha, with her obscure animosities toward Jenny; and Anna LePage, who pretends to be French as a way of liberating herself from stuffy conventions, including heterosexuality.

Patrick's supporting cast includes his roommate, Graham McClintoch, who is ugly where Patrick is handsome, awkward where Patrick is smooth. He delivers a long speech, while on a date with Jenny, about the two nations, the ugly and the good-looking, and the gulf between them. He is a bit of a dud, in Jenny's terms, but brave and chivalric in an old-fashioned way that has much to do with Jenny Bunn's own principles. More ambiguous is Julian Ormerod, an idle rich man who takes Patrick up. Ormerod begins as almost a parody of an upper-class playboy, speaking in a faded slang: "Well, there's something admirably suited for a spot of hooha, I should have thought. Now what about the old faggeroo? Eh? Let's try the old fag-o'-my-firkin" (45–46). Julian is acquainted with a variety of compliant women, to some of whom he introduces Patrick, and in general he sets a tone of easy-going hedonism. It is an important note that even he disapproves of Patrick's chosen resolution of his stalemate with Jenny.

This is the crux of the book. The plot, aside from things like cricket matches and Anna LePage's *faux* worldliness, is all about Patrick and Jenny: Patrick's desire to seduce Jenny, motivated, at least in part, by something like genuine love, resisted by Jenny's commitment to values which she holds deeply, without being able to explain them except to say that they are her values. Jenny is drawn to Patrick and tempted to give in to him. Though she considers breaking off the relationship, she cannot.

Patrick is more variable. Having begun by a semi-forceful assault, he turns next to wheedling and attempts at persuasion: "the old idea of girls being virgins when they get married" was "perfectly sensible in the days when there wasn't any birth control and they thought they could tell when a girl wasn't a virgin" (62), and besides "this is all to do with emotion, isn't it? Behaving naturally . . . " (61). From time to time, Patrick lets himself go, gives himself permission to have another woman, and this willingness to be indulgent towards himself is the key to his character. His behavior hurts Jenny, but his explanation is that she wasn't giving him what he wanted, so he had the right to get it elsewhere.

Things move toward a climax, and, at a party hosted by Julian Ormerod, where they are surrounded by drunkenness and license and women who say "that always makes things worse, making a fuss about anything to do with sex" (301), Patrick gets Jenny drunk and rapes her. That is really what it is, though (particularly decades ago, when perhaps the received idea of what counted as "seduction" was a bit more liberal), it has been read in a much more forgiving way, as for instance in James Gindin's summary: "Jenny loses her virginity, but not as a result of moral or immoral suasion; Patrick tricks her into capitulation while she is drunk."[23] The passage that describes it, from Jenny's perspective, is vague but the outlines of what happened are clear:

> Then Patrick was with her. He had been there for some minutes or hours when she first realized he was, and again was in bed with her without seeming to have got there. What he did was off by itself and nothing to do with her. All the same she wanted him to stop, but her movements were all the wrong ones for that and he was kissing her too much for her to try to tell him. She thought he would stop anyway as soon as he realized how much off on his own he was. But he did not, and did not stop, so she put her arms round him and tried to be with him, only there was no way of doing it and nothing to feel (306).

This event, based, as it seems to be, on Samuel Richardson's *Clarissa,* with its long "courtship" culminating in rape, finds its commentator when even Julian Ormerod, hitherto the exemplar of careless pleasure, objects to it. "I thought you were supposed to be in favour of all this kind of thing," Patrick pleads. "Most of it, Patty, yes. But fairness" (307).

Afterwards Jenny realizes with a new clarity Patrick's shortcomings: not only his sexual unfairness, but also his cowardice, his self-indulgence, his malice disguised as joking (he has tried to have Dick Thompson injured in a cricket match, then shot him from hiding with a pellet rifle). She denounces him, in a wonderfully crafted scene, telling him: " 'I spent too much time looking after my honour. It prevented me taking enough notice of the kind of man you are. If you are a man, *lover boy*. It's not what you did I object to; it would probably have happened anyway, sooner or later. But to do it like that' " (313).

But this is not the end. After an interlude that has no apparent relevance, except to frighten Jenny a bit about how she is perceived by her superiors at the school, there is a reconciliation with Patrick and the novel ends on a dying fall. He apologizes, after his fashion, and vows reformation; she—referring ostensibly to the loss of her "Bible-class ideas" but expressing a judgment which can easily be generalized to the whole way things have turned out—ends the novel with the words "it's rather a pity" (320). Though commentary on the novel sometimes refers to the characters' supposed decision to marry, there is no such discussion in the book. The ending is open.[24]

This novel presents readers with a greater moral challenge than any of the three that precede it. For some readers, that challenge is hidden by the expectation of humor; for others, by the "ambivalence" with which Amis indicates how they are to feel about the characters. Bernard Bergonzi claims that Patrick cannot be seen objectively, "for the author's sympathy covers him with a protective mantle of charm," while Richard Bradford argues, more cogently, that Patrick's "personal defects are really given prominence by the partial withdrawal of Amis from the shifty alliance of his earlier novels."[25] Still other readers may be confused because they agree with Patrick, and almost everyone else in the book, that virginity is not important enough to make a fuss about. But the book is not about whether or not virginity is worthwhile, but about the ethics of manipulation and responsibility, and Jenny, no matter how silly her attachment to her virginity may seem to others, has the right to her own autonomy. At the end of the book she and Patrick have an exchange about morality: he tells her (trying to console her for her loss of virginity), ''You're still the same girl. What people do doesn't change their nature,'' and Jenny sadly replies, ''What they do is their nature'' (319). This is a sobering thought for Jenny, who assumes some responsibility for doing wrong; but it is a far more damning observation about Patrick, though typically he does not see the application.

Take a Girl Like You seems to act, as one of Amis's poems puts it, ''Against Romanticism.'' Jenny's romanticism, if that is the right term for her views of love and marriage and sex and children (in that order), has been challenged by her realization that ''life had suddenly turned out to be a complicated and mysterious business'' (117). Her romanticism about making love has come up against a man who says, when Jenny asks him if it is really no more important than drinking a beer: '' 'Except that this is harder to get and the beer doesn't have to like you and you think about this more and you're proud of it afterwards and you're not supposed to have it, I suppose it is like a glass of beer. To some people. Except that this is much nicer' '' (182).

Finally, the reader's romanticism, of the sort that anticipates patterns of happy marriage, of mismatched lovers being rematched by one or both of them making a positive change, is

UNDERSTANDING KINGSLEY AMIS

challenged by the dénouement of Amis's plot. And the potential romanticism of the love plot is undone here by the realism of Jenny's discovery that Patrick is (as he sometimes sees himself) "a bastard"—after which she takes him back. *Take a Girl Like You,* particularly looked at in the long retrospect of Amis's career, is a clear milestone, a different kind of novel, a move out of a relatively pure comedy into a moral complexity touched with comedy, and a distinguished launching of his work in the 1960s.

Notes

1. Malcolm Bradbury, *No, Not Bloomsbury* (New York: Columbia University Press, 1988) 207, 204.

2. Rubin Rabinovitz, *The Reaction Against Experiment in the English Novel, 1950–1960* (New York: Columbia University Press, 1967) 4.

3. James Gindin, *Postwar British Fiction: New Accents and Attitudes* (Berkeley: University of California Press, 1963) 11.

4. David Lodge, *Write On: Occasional Essays '65–'85* (London: Secker and Warburg, 1986) 63–64.

5. Walter Allen, *Tradition and Dream: The English and American Novel from the Twenties to Our Time* (London: Phoenix House, 1964) 280.

6. Martin Green, "British Decency," *Kenyon Review* 21 (Autum 1959): 531. Leavis dismissed Amis as a "pornographer" when Amis was given a fellowship at Cambridge in 1961. See Kingsley Amis, *Memoirs* (New York: Summit Books, 1991) 217. For some more of the many attempts to define the new kind of hero created by Amis, see Gindin 43; J. D. Scott, "Britain's Angry Young Men," *The Saturday Review* 40 (July 27, 1957): 9; Derek Colville, "The Sane New World of Kingsley Amis," *Bucknell Review* 9 (March 1960): 48; William Van O'Connor, "Two Types of 'Heroes' in Post-War British Fiction," *PMLA* 77 (March 1962): 168; and John McDermott, *Kingsley Amis: An English Moralist* (New York: St. Martin's, 1989) 25.

AMIS'S NOVELS IN THE 1950s

7. Rabinovitz 52; Harold Orel, "The Decline and Fall of a Comic Novelist: Kingsley Amis," *Kansas Quarterly* 1 (Summer 1969): 17.

8. Walker Gibson, " 'You Musn't Say Things Like That,' " *The Nation* 187 (November 29, 1958): 410.

9. Amis, *Memoirs* 56.

10. Kingsley Amis, *Lucky Jim* (Garden City, NY: Doubleday, 1954) 41. Further references will be noted parenthetically in the text.

11. McDermott 67.

12. David Lodge, *Language of Fiction: Essays in Criticism and Verbal Analysis of the English Novel* (New York: Columbia University Press, 1966) 255.

13. Bradbury 209. See also Norman Macleod, *"This Familiar Regressive Series:* Aspects of Style in the Novels of Kingsley Amis," in *Edinburgh Studies in English and Scots,* ed. A. J. Aitken et al. (London: Longman, 1971) 121–43.

14. Kingsley Amis, *That Uncertain Feeling* (New York: Harcourt, Brace, 1956) 35. Further references will be noted parenthetically in the text.

15. Michael Barber, "The Art of Fiction LIX: Kingsley Amis," *Paris Review* 64 (1975): 48.

16. Richard J. Voorhees, "Three Hurrahs and a Reservation," *Queens Quarterly* 74 (Spring 1972): 38; John D. Hurrell, "Class and Conscience in John Braine and Kingsley Amis," *Critique* 2 (1958–59): 50.

17. Norman Macleod, "A Trip to Greeneland: The Plagiarizing Narrator of Kingsley Amis's *I Like It Here,*" *Studies in the Novel* 17 (Summer 1985): 207; Robert H. Hopkins, "The Satire of Kingsley Amis's *I Like It Here,*" *Critique* 8 (Spring/Summer 1966): 63; cf. Green, in "British Decency," who makes Amis a fellow examplar, *along with* Leavis, of the traits he praises.

18. Kingsley Amis, *I Like It Here* (New York: Harcourt, Brace, 1958) 29. Further references will be noted parenthetically in the text.

19. Lodge, *Language of Fiction* 261. Cf. McDermott 96.

20. Terry Teachout, "A Touch of Class," *The New Criterion* 7 (November 1988): 12.

21. McDermott 109.

22. Kingsley Amis, *Take a Girl Like You* (New York: Harcourt, Brace & World, 1961) 49. Further references will be noted parenthetically in the text.

23. Gindin *Postwar British Fiction,* 40–41.

24. James Gindin writes that "the novels are never open-ended," and though his essay purports to include *Take a Girl Like You,* he is wrong on the

indeterminacy of its conclusion: "Well Beyond Laughter: Directions from Fifties' Comic Fiction," *Studies in the Novel* 3 (Winter 1971): 361.

25. Bernard Bergonzi, *The Situation of the Novel* (Pittsburgh: University of Pittsburgh Press, 1970) 166; Richard Bradford, *Kingsley Amis* (London: Edward Arnold, 1989) 43.

CHAPTER THREE

Poetry and Miscellaneous Nonfiction

In a 1975 interview with Dale Salwak, Amis accepted a description of himself as a "man of letters," which he defined this way:

I think of myself like a sort of mid- or late-Victorian person, not in outlook but in the position of writing a bit of poetry (we forget that George Eliot also wrote verse), writing novels, being interested in questions of the day and occasionally writing about them, and being interested in the work of other writers and occasionally writing about that.[1]

He is undoubtedly best known as a novelist; that more than anything else is his work, and this book is mostly about Kingsley Amis the novelist. But his achievement in the other fields suggested by the term "man of letters" is significant, too.

Poetry

Though his verse appeared in a variety of minor ways during the 1950s, there are four major books of poetry by

Kingsley Amis. The first, *Bright November,* appeared in 1947; in 1957 Victor Gollancz (a mainline house, for a change) published a much larger collection, *A Case of Samples: Poems, 1946–1956,* which included six of the thirty-one poems from *Bright November; A Look Round the Estate: Poems 1957–1967* appeared in 1968; and the contents of these books were supplemented by later work in *Collected Poems: 1944–1979.*

Throughout his career, Amis has been a poet devoted to use of traditional formal devices in poetry; his poems rhyme and scan, and he makes good use of *terza rima* and challenging forms like the villanelle. Sometimes critics claim membership for him in "The Movement," a postwar trend in English poetry, that might best be defined as anti-Modernist, anti-Romantic, dedicated to clarity of thought and feeling and a return to the main lines of English verse, including rhyme and meter. Patricia Ball identifies the Movement aim as "to speak of things as they are—especially the ugly and horrible" and insists that it is "our venerated, hackneyed, abused but enduring norm for creative work and the criticism of it."[2] One of the reasons for Amis's hostility to Dylan Thomas—aside from his unpleasant encounter with him in person—is that Amis thinks that Thomas's work crystallizes pretty much everything against which Amis's poetry strives: grandiosity, pretentiousness, obscurity, avant-gardism for its own sake, and perversity of thought and emotion. Amis, like his good friend Philip Larkin, seems to want a poetry that is sensible and normally sensitive.

It is by no means a crude or lowbrow poetry (though some of the recent poems in the 1979 collection tend in this

POETRY AND MISCELLANEOUS NONFICTION

direction). Amis has always had his admirers, among whom there have been voices predicting that he would soon assume his place in the foreground of contemporary poetry. Something has clearly stopped this placement. No doubt, it is partly his increasing absorption in public controversy, his focus on fiction, and (perhaps) the hardening of positions, with an accompanying decline in subtlety, of the poems of the seventies. He also seems to write less poetry. *A Case of Samples* collects the output of 1946–1956, and contains forty-five poems even though most of *Bright November* is omitted; *A Look Round the Estate,* from 1957–1967, has thirty-five; and the poems from 1968 to 1979 in *Collected Poems* number only twenty-three, many of them very short, epitaphs in fact.

The early Amis poetry has an echo of W. H. Auden, with a combination of elevated language and clever phrasing and sometimes deflating wit. "Against Romanticism"—a title that sums up much of his poetic program—is a complex meditation on man's aspiration for something wilder than reality, man's inability to be satisfied with "a temperate zone."[3] "A Bookshop Idyll" distinguishes between the sexes on the basis of poems written by male and female poets, the men insisting by their titles on the value of thought, travel, learning; the women, on love. The speaker concludes that men can get along (at least in their poetry) without love, but women cannot, and leads on to the conclusion that "Women are really much nicer than men . . . " (57). There are poems here that celebrate love and beauty, but Amis's distinctive voice is really most in evidence in poems which examine or deflate the false. For instance, "Beowulf" makes fun, not of that work but of the exaggerated claims for its greatness, in a poem flecked with phrases from the classroom ("discuss and illustrate" "weak conjugation" [18]).

The same themes appear in *A Look Round the Estate,* with the added change of a slangier, more demotic style. These poems are likely to lead to perceptions like "Change is for kids" (75). Disappointment is very much the note in many of these poems. "New Approach Needed" is addressed to Christ, and concludes by advising him: "next time, come off it" (90). The last section of *A Look Round the Estate* is a collection of poems, previously published separately as *The Evans Country,* about a small-town seducer, Dai Evans, in Aberdarcy, Amis's fictional Welsh locale. It is a grim, modern country of grime and ugliness and tawdry, meaningless sex, quite up to *The Waste Land* (not that Amis would count that as a compliment) in distaste for the people and places it depicts. "St. Asaph's" parodies Yeats's "Among School Children," showing that in this case, Evans's interest in school children is strictly sexual. "Aldport (Mystery Tour)" shows Dai, explaining to himself how reverent tourists gaze at The Parthenon through sunglasses by remembering touching up a woman, "outside The Gents," while wearing gloves (114). The poems about Evans are brilliant; they leave a sour taste, but they are meant to, and at times the speaker rounds on the reader to demand that he question his assumption of superiority to Evans.

In the decade's worth of new poems in *Collected Poems,* disillusionment, along with a sharper interest in death and disease and aging, come to the fore. There are lines here which

POETRY AND MISCELLANEOUS NONFICTION

voice Amis's quasi-political anger against the 1960s and 1970s, lines about the ruin of education, the decay of language, the near future of universal, "unchangeable crappiness" (134). "Their Oxford" echoes the phrase "my Oxford" while repudiating it, and details changes for the worse in Amis's *alma mater;* "Farewell Blues" is about what "they" have done to ruin jazz; and "Shitty" is a sort of all-purpose jeremiad against "all things shitty" including everything from rock singers to performances of Samuel Beckett at the Institute for Contemporary Arts (122). The dismissal is not exactly redeemed by the affirmation that even these things, "shitty" as they are, are more lovely than the screens around the bed of a (presumably dying) hospital patient.

There is humor in this collection of poems. Amis writes with his old sting and with an undiluted skill with forms, but the morbidity, the insistent rage against the modern, and the impatient lumping together of all kinds of "unchangeable crappiness" including modern clothing styles, senility, dying, and German tourists, works against the delicacy and more credible feeling (though less vehemently expressed) of the poems of the first two collections.

Literary Criticism

Amis has written three books of literary criticism, in addition to substantial amounts of it contained in the books he has edited. Though he was university lecturer in English for a dozen years, he has written almost no "academic" criticism.

His critical books are occasional—for instance, arising out
American lectures or his background reading for a novel—and
typically they focus on authors or genres that are intellectually
suspect, popular but "lowbrow"—science fiction, the James
Bond books, and Rudyard Kipling.

When Amis was in residence at Princeton in 1958–59,
one of the conditions of the position was giving a series of lectures on literature, the Gauss Seminars. At the suggestion of
R. P. Blackmur, he lectured on the then-surprising topic of science fiction. As he reports, these lectures by 1960 "had become a book, *New Maps of Hell,* which was to make quite a
sizeable contribution to the raising of science fiction to the
status of a branch of culture, or 'culture,' and so to its eventual
undoing."[4]

In *New Maps of Hell* (1960), Amis writes as a science-
fiction *fan.* He deplores the interest then beginning to be taken
in science fiction by "trend-hounds" and literary critics who
read the genre for its symbolism. He represents the point of
view of those who read it because of the pleasure—the excite-
ment—it gives them.

He develops an interesting analogy between science fiction and jazz (long an Amis love), pointing out, perhaps more
breezily than accurately, that both developed in America in the
1930s; both "have strong connections with mass culture without being, as I hope to show in the case of science fiction,
mass media in themselves"; both "have thrown up a large
number of interesting and competent figures without producing anybody of first-rate importance"; and (most ominously)
"both jazz and science fiction have in the last dozen years be-

POETRY AND MISCELLANEOUS NONFICTION

gun to attract the attention of the cultural diagnostician, or trend-hound, who becomes interested in them not for or as themselves, but for the light they can be made to throw on some other thing.''[5] This book is hardly a systematic study of science fiction, partly because Amis was limited to discussing books he bought and borrowed in America and partly because, as a sort of representative of the common reader, he would likely find a ''systematic study'' to be the work of the cultural diagnostician. It is interesting and lively and, at least according to Amis, apparently is the first serious academic treatment of science fiction.

In the mid-1960s, Amis was immersed in Ian Fleming's books about James Bond, with two results. One is his own James Bond novel (*Colonel Sun,* 1968), written after Ian Fleming's death; the other is his second book of literary criticism, *The James Bond Dossier* (1965). The book might best be seen as a defense of the James Bond books and a celebration of Bond himself. Amis defends him, not uncritically, but from a sort of middlebrow perspective, against charges of cruelty, sadism, sexism, and so on. Amis shows a very close familiarity with the Bond books. Here there is a good bit of waspishness about ''the critics'' and their obtuseness and picayune objections, and much celebration of the *joy* of reading, and the harmless pleasure of identifying with James Bond. Throughout the book, Amis makes it clear that he rejoices to concur with the common reader.

Of more interest, or at least more applicability beyond the Bond oeuvre, are his comments in an appendix on ''Literature and Escape.'' Here he argues that ''all literature is escapist.''

He makes an intelligent claim that escapism includes not just simple identification but the use of literature (and other arts, by the way) to console: "One of the qualities that took us to it in the first place is its implicit assurance that life is coherent and meaningful, and I can think of no more escapist notion than that." He goes on to quote Matthew Arnold on the consolatory function of poetry and concludes with a judgment that helps to explain why his own extended criticism is all about non-elite writers and works:

> Let me admit at once that even if we take for granted the fusion of escapist and enlightening elements in art, we can still point to plenty of works in which one or the other predominates, and I'm in no doubt about which end of the spectrum is occupied by the adventures of 007. But I do want it thought of as a spectrum, not as a ladder or a class list, and 007's end of it hasn't been studied enough. Fiction written and read primarily for escape isn't necessarily devoid of the virtues in which primarily enlightening fiction is rich, and escape fiction can have virtues much of its own as well. There's not a lot of suspense in the classics.[6]

Rudyard Kipling and His World (1975) is part of a series called "Thames and Hudson Literary Lives." It contains biography of Kipling, drawn from published sources (Amis readily disavows any real pretense of originality or new research), discussion of the books, and 114 illustrations. As in *The James Bond Dossier,* this is partly a defense. Amis sets out, without attempting to whitewash them, Kipling's racism, imperialism, and paternalism; he does attempt to contextualize them for a juster judgment.

POETRY AND MISCELLANEOUS NONFICTION

It is hard to know exactly what sort of audience this book might be for; it is certainly too sketchy for a serious student, but, when Amis begins criticizing Kipling's works, he seems to assume a familiarity with them which a beginner would not have. At any rate, it does have a number of nice touches, among them the rather pompous statement that (of some intellectual shortcoming of Kipling's): "A course of study at Oxford or Cambridge would have put things right, but both roads to it were closed."[7] Other comments have the sting that makes Amis's criticism almost always worth reading. Henry James was baffled by Kipling's choice of a wife, and Amis comments, "Some might mutter that to mystify James over some piece of normal human behaviour was no great feat" (66).

Miscellaneous Nonfiction

Amis's interest in the work of other writers and in the issues of his day, and his writing about them, have resulted in a large amount of miscellaneous journalism. Much of this, and presumably the best of it, is collected in two books: *What Became of Jane Austen? And Other Questions* (1970) and *The Amis Collection: Selected Non-Fiction 1954–1990* (1990). Each of these collections, of which the second is much weightier, contains many book reviews along with essays on social questions, autobiographical pieces and expressions of personal opinion (often grievance), and some odd things like an essay "On Christ's Nature."

An unsystematic survey of the contents of *What Became of Jane Austen?* indicates the range of Amis's interests. Terry

Teachout writes, not unjustly, that "the journalistic Amis is to some extent a theatrical creation, a beef-eating pantomime Englishman who, for all his untutored literary shrewdness . . . is also a perfectly sincere fan of genre fiction."[8] There are sympathetic treatments of unfashionable authors: Kipling, Jules Verne, Ian Fleming, Erle Stanley Gardner, and other authors of detective fiction. There are scathing treatments of fashionable authors or fashionable types of writing: Dylan Thomas, Vladimir Nabokov, Philip Roth (particularly *Portnoy's Complaint*, which Amis never tires of abominating), Arnold Wesker, and Colin Wilson. In the area of social commentary, the richest vein is mined in an essay called "Why Lucky Jim Turned Right," written in 1967 and explaining what must have seemed, to those who saw Amis and Jim Dixon as embodiments of 1950s radicalism, the apostasy of the author's increasing hatred of the British Labour Party. (The publisher's title of this essay unfortunately helps to foster the simplistic identification of Kingsley Amis and his most famous character which elsewhere he has been at pains to discourage; Lucky Jim never turned right, or did anything else beyond the last page of *Lucky Jim*.) Amis's main complaints against the Labour party center on its foreign policy (not anti-Communist enough) and its education policies (anti-intellectual, foolishly egalitarian, trendy). There are a few bits of autobiography here as well, including a sympathetic memoir of the author's father and some pieces about his education and his time in Wales.

By 1990 things had changed very much for Amis. The very title of the most recent collection—*The Amis Collec-*

tion—announces the confidence of Amis or his publishers. And this one not only issues from an author now become almost a national institution but also covers almost forty years of journalism as well. No wonder it is imposing. The choice of topics is a good bit like that in *What Became of Jane Austen?* There are many book reviews, again often skewering the fashionable (Dylan Thomas again, Max Beerbohm), praising Kipling and the authors of the unfashionable genres, like science fiction and detective stories. He is more open about praising people known to be his friends, including the novelists Elizabeth Taylor and Anthony Powell and poet Philip Larkin. He writes interestingly on language and music and on foreign travel, and his many reviews of poetry anthologies are glosses on the three anthologies he edited during the period. There is much less autobiography, except for incidental bits in reviews, which is probably to be explained by the almost simultaneous publication of his *Memoirs* (1991), a book which in fact incorporates much that appeared in *What Became of Jane Austen* as occasional essays. On the other hand, Amis's increasing preoccupation with social questions comes more clearly to the fore, with a good bit of anti-feminism here, a larger amount about public subsidy for the arts (he is vehemently opposed to it), and a great deal on education. His efforts here, often co-authored with his friend Robert Conquest, a minor poet and distinguished writer on the Soviet Union, are part of a public campaign against "progressive" educational policy in Britain, particularly in the Inner London Education Authority, and are heavy-handed "satires," which are obviously meant to amuse but are, finally, too shrill to do so.

UNDERSTANDING KINGSLEY AMIS

A thorough reading of this impressive collection creates two primary impressions: one of them is of a conservative man reacting strongly to what he sees as regressive trends in fiction, language, social arrangements, and much more. These reactions may usually be seen as reasonable conclusions from his well-known premises; for instance, his conviction that fiction should be lucid and accessible to ordinary readers will *always* lead him to disdain mandarin writing or preciosity. The second lasting impression is of Amis's energy, wide-range curiosity, and learning. He writes as well on Tennyson as he does on Jelly Roll Morton, as confidently on eighteenth-century verse as on James Bond. That Amis writes most amusingly and vigorously when on the attack is no disgrace, for, after all, it is true of most critics, and he is on the attack much of the time. The results are incisive pieces which (like his novels) start with a snap. For instance: "The trouble with nonsense is that any fool can write it and any one bit of it is as good or bad or indifferent as any other" or "Deciding which is the most boring long poem in English is, even given the existence of *Piers Plowman,* by no means an easy task."[9] Amis's essays will never cause people to overlook his fiction, but they are consistently interesting and often a real joy to read.

Autobiography

In 1991 Kingsley Amis published his *Memoirs.* Preceded by much discussion in the press of their daring revelations and wicked insight into English literary life in the past forty years,

POETRY AND MISCELLANEOUS NONFICTION

publication was followed by quite a bit of disappointment and head-wagging. *Memoirs* is indeed an odd sort of performance. It consists, as he explains, ''not of a connected narrative but of a series of essays or sketches,'' most of them about other people.[10] Thus the chapters often bear titles like ''Anthony Powell'' or ''Robert Graves.'' Others are about places which also figure as phases in Amis's life, like Oxford or the USA (his two periods of residency), or about topics that are neither people nor places, including booze and jazz. Even the arrangement of chapters lacks chronological necessity, though family and schools precede the chapters about the friends of his maturity or about Margaret Thatcher.

There are odd omissions. There is really very little here about writing, for instance (*The Amis Collection* is better on that topic). And the treatment of his marriages is odd indeed. The facts, of when he married Hilary and Jane, are studiously elided, as is the aftermath of his second divorce, which led to a sort of reconciliation with Hilary. Hilary leads the roster of dedicatees, and the book concludes with a poem to and about her called ''Instead of an Epilogue.''

Still, having titled his book *Memoirs* instead of *My Life* or *Autobiography,* Amis is entitled to such inclusions and omissions as he likes. What is more troubling about this book is the mean-spiritedness of some of it. Many of the chapters tell of encounters with famous people whom Amis did not like, portraying their stupidity or drunkenness or lechery or racism or (most often) tight-fistedness in cruel vignettes. There are exceptions, in the cases of friends like Peter Quennell and Anthony Powell, who are generally praised. But even some of those Amis likes look bad here. His friend Robert Conquest, whom Amis writes about approvingly but whose wife he puts in a bad light, has protested the accuracy of the book, and some reviewers disliked the treatment of Amis's "best friend" Philip Larkin. Recounting a fairly disgusting occasion when the drunken Larkin urinated in his suit seems hard to justify on any grounds, including the fact that Larkin is now dead.

Craig Brown, reviewing the *Memoirs* in the *Times Literary Supplement,* comments on the harshness, the long memory of those who failed to buy their round of drinks some time in the 1950s, and suggests a possible reason for Amis's waspish tone: "Given the widespread view that Amis's first novel was also his best . . . it seems that the special care he takes to beat up those contemporaries whose bright futures now lie behind them could be a means of bolstering his own success, of rubbing that knighthood and those sales in their mouths, lest they question how far he, too, has progressed."[11]

There are good things in the *Memoirs.* For instance, Amis's chapter on his time at Vanderbilt University provides good background for understanding *I Want It Now,* as the material on Princeton does for *One Fat Englishman.* Of deeper import are his comments on psychoanalysis, a topic of great importance in novels like *Jake's Thing* and *Stanley and the Women.* On the one hand, there is this on analysis: "Freudianism has probably been instrumental in fewer deaths than Nazism or Marxism, though it is surely one of the great pernicious doctrines of our century with its denial of free will and personal responsibility" (117). On the other, there is a very interesting account of Amis's own emotional problems with vague dreads, agoraphobia, and hallucinations and a spotty record of treatment by psychologists, which shows that the treatment of mental therapy in the novels is not just drawn from outside observation. Despite these contributions to a better understanding of Amis the novelist, and occasional passages of fine writing, *Memoirs* fails to be either an uninteresting *but crucial* book, or an unimportant *but entertaining* one.

Notes

1. Dale Salwak, "An Interview with Kingsley Amis," *Contemporary Literature* 16 (1975): 18.

2. Patricia Ball, "The Photographic Art," *Review of English Literature* 3 (April 1962): 50.

3. Kingsley Amis, *Collected Poems 1944–1979* (New York: Viking Press, 1981): 36. All quotations of poetry are from this edition.

4. Kingsley Amis, *Memoirs* (New York: Summit Books, 1991) 210.

5. Kingsley Amis, *New Maps of Hell* (New York: Harcourt, Brace & World, 1960) 17–18.

6. Kingsley Amis, *The James Bond Dossier* (New York: New American Library, 1965) 137, 138.

7. Kingsley Amis, *Rudyard Kipling and His World* (New York: Scribners, 1975) 31.

8. Terry Teachout, "A Touch of Class," *The New Criterion* 7 (November 1988): 13.

9. Kingsley Amis, *The Amis Collection: Selected Non-Fiction 1954–1990* (London: Hutchinson, 1990) 152, 179.

10. Amis, *Memoirs* xv.

11. Craig Brown, "Amis Buys His Round of Poison: Blokeish Bad Humour from the Lounge Bar," *Times Literary Supplement* 8 March 1991: 9.

CHAPTER FOUR

The 1960s

Kingsley Amis's novels in the 1960s continued to trace the arc established by his work in the 1950s. The books continued to be comic, predominantly, but with a darkening tone. Though they continued to have at their center characters whose morality is challenged by the events they face, particularly the morality of relationships between men and women, the novels also concern themselves with more specific themes. Clive James certainly oversimplifies, but there is something to his summary of Amis's books in a 1974 profile: "With Amis the theme always does [emerge], whether it is being your own man (*Lucky Jim*) or faithfulness (*That Uncertain Feeling/Only Two Can Play*) or Abroad (*I Like It Here*) or virginity (*Take a Girl Like You*) or swinishness (*One Fat Englishman*) or the necessity to kill (*The Anti-Death League*) or the limits of ambition (*I Want It Now*) or the reality of love and evil (*The Green Man*). . . . "[1] Is "swinishness" a *theme?* Perhaps. Certainly, *One Fat Englishman* poses questions about swinish behavior, the demands it makes on other people, and the prospects for happiness and even success of the swinish.

THE 1960s

There is something very much of the period in Amis's mainstream novels of the 1960s. In *One Fat Englishman*, there is an incisive exploration of the anti-Americanism, compounded of unequal parts of snobbery, resentment, recognition of genuine deficiencies, and perhaps envy, which formed an important part of the English ethos in that decade. *The Anti-Death League* is a sensitive study of love and death played out against a background of cold war tensions and the development of horrific weapons of war. *I Want It Now* investigates the lives, including the pains as well as the dubious joys, of the very rich and of media superstars, and by taking another turn in the United States, this time the South, attacks racism. *The Green Man*, though the least obviously topical of this group—it is a ghost story—looks at, or critiques, the fashionable faithlessness of the 1960s.

In this period, also, Amis began his versatile experimentation in genre fiction and unusual methods of composition; *The Egyptologists* (1965) is an effort in collaboration with Robert Conquest, and a somewhat tricky narrative, too; *Colonel Sun* is a James Bond book, published under a pseudonym. These will be treated in chapter 5, which looks at short stories and genre fiction.

One Fat Englishman (1963)

Roger Micheldene, the title character of *One Fat Englishman*, may be seen as Amis's decisive declaration of independence from his own protagonists. It has always been not only possible but necessary to see that the leading male characters of the novels *are not Kingsley Amis;* but this necessity has not meant that readers have always kept the distinction in mind. It is too easy to see Jim Dixon as Amis, particularly when one knows that some of his circumstances and some of his opinions are shared with his author. Thus critics transfer the "filthy Mozart" attitude to Amis, giving him, along the way, Dixon's personal history, class position, and so on. This is wrong, but it is seductive. Even more wrong but still seductive is the confusion of the author with John Lewis, or Garnet Bowen, or Patrick Standish, all of them witty men, literary intellectuals, whose attitudes to, say, drinking, Welshness, and modern literature are often those of Amis.

Such an identification dulls the reader's ability to notice that these men are progressively more intolerant, lazy, wrongheaded about women. Readers are meant to take the measure of them, and to do so they must see them as created characters, often exposed to sharp satire or revealed as mean or even contemptible, not as avatars of the author. Amis's characters increasingly *are,* and often know themselves to be, "awful" men—that is, immoral, selfish, sexually rapacious. Amis's novels often refer to a character as a "bastard" or a "shit" as a sort of shorthand citation of these character flaws. Roger Micheldene is clearly one of Amis's "bastards."

Reading Amis's tone, trying to understand how we ought to react to the characters, is, as always, not simple. As usual, it is even harder for readers who are trying to read *One Fat Englishman,* or Amis's later works generally, as a sort of pal-

THE 1960s

impsest, beneath all of which is always and forever *Lucky Jim*. Leslie Paul thinks the fat Englishman, Roger Micheldene, may be "Jim Dixon a decade or so down the line," while Kenneth Hamilton concludes that Roger's nemesis, Irving Macher, is "an American Jim Dixon, who is not vulnerable."[2] (Maybe *nobody* in this novel is Jim Dixon?)

Very likely one reason for making Roger Micheldene "one fat Englishman" (the phrase is used by a woman who is recuperating from a sexual bout with him) is to help readers distance him. Roger has many characteristics, in addition to being fat, that mark him off from the typical Amis protagonist and from Amis. Though a publisher, he hates reading and writers; he has a variety of obnoxious affectations, including snuff-taking and elaborate fault-finding with any but the most expensive cigars. In short he is swinish. As Clive James comments, "Micheldene's swinishness is a device meant to discredit the opinions he holds."[3] Among these are anti-Semitism, misogyny, and anti-Americanism.

It may be a sign of the times that many readers have taken *One Fat Englishman* as an anti-American novel. Though the Americans in it are by no means universally charming or wise, the anti-Americanism is largely the contribution of Roger, who is, after all, awful in almost all his beliefs and behavior. He thinks pungently about this country: "The distance of the houses from one another, their wooden construction, the absence of horticulture and fences or walls, the woodland setting, all combined to give the area [an upper-middle-class suburb in a place like Princeton, New Jersey] the look of a semi-temporary encampment for a battalion of parvenus. Not a bad image of America as a whole, eh?''[4] But Amis has carefully constructed Roger's character so as to deny him ''authority.''

This is slightly complicated by the fact that, though impossibly swinish, Roger is still (somehow and sometimes) likable. Amis himself concedes that, though ''Roger is undoubtedly the most unpleasant of my leading characters'' up to this point, ''I like Roger.''[5] Some characters in the novel like him, others want his approval, and he is not unsuccessful sexually. But everybody likes people while disapproving of them, and Roger Micheldene is a representative of much that, Amis suggests, needs reproof and correction. Which explains why the plot is devoted to the exposure, humiliation, and frustration of this fat Englishman. Roger's situation opens him to attack on various fronts: his profession, his self-esteem, his national pride, his ordinary relations with others, his sex life. On all of these fronts, he is bested.

In America for a few days on publishing business, Roger has one major aim, to reestablish sexual relations with his former mistress, Helene Bang. Her husband, a linguist, has a teaching position at Budweiser College. Roger's sexual ambitions require him to be fairly tolerant of a variety of people who annoy him and whom he would like to affront openly; in fact, he fantasizes about violence against them with great gusto. ''Say no more. Or else stand by for a dose of grievous bodily harm (Roger thought to himself), you women's-cultural-lunch-club-organizing *Saturday Review of Literature*-reading substantial-inheritance-from-soft-drink-corporation-awaiting old-New-Hampshire-family-invoking Kennedy-loving justwunnerful-labelling Yank bag'' (24). Roger doesn't actually attack people physically, though he thinks about it enough. He does insult people, usually those who offend him by blandness or enthusiasm.

His pursuit of Helene is complicated in a variety of ways. There are the ordinary events which make adultery difficult—children about, husband in the way, Helene's unwillingness to compromise herself. What becomes increasingly apparent to the reader, though not to Roger, is that Helene does not want to sleep with Roger, despite his ambushes and bullying demands.

The other major character in *One Fat Englishman* is Irving Macher, a young Jewish American writer who is at the same time a student at Budweiser College, the author of a novel called *Blinkie Heaven,* and a sort of sexual rival of Roger's. From the beginning, Macher gets under Roger's skin by being coolly unimpressed by him and by his superior irony. He further infuriates him by mischievous interventions. When Roger is invited to lecture at the college (an occasion on which he expects to impress Helene), Macher steals his lecture script from his briefcase and substitutes a copy of *Crazy* magazine. In a humorless huff, Roger refuses to give the lecture and accuses Helene's little boy of having made the switch. Here as elsewhere, Irving Macher functions as Roger's nemesis, a role he has assigned himself. As he explains, ''my role—in your life, that is—is to give you chances of behaving naturally, that's to say not in prefabricated sections, not out of some shooting script but off the cuff'' (132).

Further agony derives from Roger Micheldene's discovery that Macher's *Blinkie Heaven* is not, as he has not only wished but actually prayed to God—for Roger is a believing though inconsistently practicing Catholic—a bad novel. It isn't good, but he recognizes that it will be published and will sell; even more baffling, it isn't what he thinks of as a typical American novel: "There were blind people, true, and the odd Negro, but they were not backed up by the expected paraplegic necrophiles, hippoerotic jockeys, exhibitionistic castrates, coprophagic pig-farmers, armless flagellationists and the rest of the bunch. . . . Events took place and the reader could determine what they were. There was spoken dialogue, appearing between quotation marks" (75).

Roger's progress, if that is the right word, through his American days is marked by an almost eerie self-destructiveness. If he is really in love with Helene, it is odd that he is so easily side-tracked by a woman called Mollie Atkins, with whom he has impromptu sex on the lawn during a party and later, again out of doors in the daytime, where he is frightened by a tortoise. Later at a party he permits himself to believe that Irving Macher's girl friend is interested in him—hurting Mollie Atkins, along the way, by his attentions—and seems surprised when the girl gives him a painful bite; the only explanation he can conceive for this is that she is a lesbian.

Roger's "love" for Helene is even more often and more easily sidetracked by his anger, always disproportionate to the occasion, as in the case of the purloined lecture notes and his fulminations against a Catholic priest. In the dénouement, Helene reveals her disgust for Roger and admits that she went to bed with him out of pity. Moreover she explains quite cogently:

"You don't like me."

"Helene, I love you. I love you and I want to marry you."

"Maybe you do, but you don't like me." (186)

This follows the development that neatly ties together Roger's two main preoccupations in a way maximally punitive to him: Helene goes away, not with Roger, as she has promised, but with Irving Macher. Clearly, he is a more attractive person than Roger: but clearly there is also an element here of Helene's striking at Roger in the way which will be most painful.

Everything having collapsed, Roger retreats to England. He has one consolation, having stolen a manuscript notebook of Swinburne's from an American who, by his thinking, has no right to such an English treasure. Even his journey "among one's own people" (the English crew) is contaminated by his discovery that Strode Atkins, the most obnoxious American he has met and the husband of the accessible Mollie, is his traveling companion (191). The novel ends with the promise of Strode talking all the way across the Atlantic.

A very funny book, *One Fat Englishman* is also very pointed. Amis, who has commented often on Roger Micheldene, explains that he "is a bastard to a very large extent, and he understands it and yet he can't be different. One isn't asking for sympathy for him exactly, but we all have our crosses to bear, and being a bastard and realizing it is a kind of cross which he bears. Right at the end, the author steps forward, so to speak, to sympathize with Roger, and Roger weeps because although nobody says so, he was actually in love with Helene, or loved her as much as he is capable of loving anybody, and now he's lost her."[6]

The book punishes Roger for being so awful—he loses everything that is important to him, including something even more important than Helene, which is his conviction of his own superiority, particularly to Irving Macher. But it invites the reader to see as well that bastards suffer, too. Perhaps the mishaps become excessive, the Furies do their job too well. The writing in *One Fat Englishman* is complex; the tone is finely managed; and the resulting mixture of pleasure and pain, laughter and pity, disapproval and empathy testifies to Amis's art.

The Anti-Death League (1966)

Here is a novel reminiscent of *Take a Girl Like You*, despite their very different subjects. It is bigger, broader, more ambitious, more complex than the ones it follows and precedes. It isn't without humor, but the humor is toned well down. The themes are serious. *Take a Girl Like You*, despite Clive James's handy summary, isn't on the "theme" of virginity; Jenny's virginity is the site of activity on a much more important theme: human freedom and integrity, and the assault on it by one's own emotions and less scrupulous people. *The Anti-Death League* is about love and death. One of the sobering qualities of it, by contrast with Amis's work up to this point, is that in it a good many people do die, mostly in apparently meaningless ways, and others are threatened with death.

Like three of Amis's good early short stories, this book is set among noncombatant soldiers. There is a sharp tension here, though, deriving from the fact that these men are involved in the top-secret "Project Apollo," which clearly has to do with a weapon of advanced destructiveness. The suggestion through the book is that it is nuclear. Within this setting, with its heightened attentions to loyalty and betrayal and the possibilities of espionage, Amis uses the officers and those related to them to explore a variety of serious themes.

The central figure may be James Churchill, who is involved in an important love affair; or Max Hunter, who is actually behind the "Anti-Death League"; or Brian Leonard, the semi-competent spy-catcher; or Willie Ayscue, the chaplain whose heroism consists of overcoming his lack of Christian faith; or even Moti Naidu, the Asian officer who seems to speak most reasonably about life and death.

Death and the threat of death permeate this novel. Near the beginning a motorcycle rider carrying dispatches dies meaninglessly in a road accident. At the very end, Ayscue's faithful dog is killed in another meaningless road accident. An enlisted man dies horribly of a sudden meningitis. James Churchill, struggling to come to terms with his lover's breast cancer, puts forward an elegant explanation, though it is hard to know how seriously Amis offers it for our belief:

You've probably heard of these things they call lethal nodes. . . . Well, we're in a lethal node now, only it's one that works in time instead of space. A bit of life it's death to enter. The beginning, the edge of the node was when that motor-cycle thing happened. Fawkes was further in. This looks like being near the centre. We'll know it's passing over when somebody else goes, somebody we know as little as we knew that dispatch-rider. That'll be the farther edge. I know all this sounds a bit mad. I'm sorry.[7]

In one of Amis's little jokes, "somebody else" who goes is L. S. Caton, a familiar name through all his early novels, beginning with *Lucky Jim*, where he steals Jim's article and publishes it under his own name in an Argentinian journal. Named for some reason after Amis's first publisher, Caton is always writing from a distance, promising to do something "in due course" or "before very long," and never doing it. Having him die in a horrible way in *The Anti-Death League* satisfies the needs of the lethal node concept while (perhaps) ridding Amis of a device he was tired of.

Each of the major characters in the book is anti-death. The irony of this (since they are all professionally devoted to the infliction of death) is not lost on them, and in fact only Churchill becomes opposed to Operation Apollo, which is designed to kill millions. Churchill's conversion arises from falling in love with Catherine Casement, another of the attractive and good heroines in the same line with Christine Callaghan and Jenny Bunn, then discovering that Catherine has cancer. He "just got angry at the way good things are vulnerable to bad things, but bad things aren't vulnerable to good" (192). Finally, he becomes almost comatose, resisting through passivity his involvement in a world which includes Catherine's illness and Project Apollo.

A similar reaction occurs with Max Hunter, a brother officer who is being treated for alcoholism. He is an unhappy homosexual (treated with complete sympathy despite some insensitive treatment of "queers" in some of Amis's other books) whose stimulus to rebellion is the meaningless death of Fawkes, who is the friend of Pearce, an enlisted man Hunter is interested in. As Churchill's rebellion is passive, Hunter's is furtive, taking the form of anonymous manifestos and poems against death—not against killing but death itself. His poem "To A Baby Born Without Limbs" is the sharpest protest in the novel against what seems a casual malevolence in God or the universe.

Two religious perspectives on death are offered by Ayscue, the Christian priest, and Moti, who seems to be a Buddhist. Ayscue insists that "to believe at all deeply in the Christian God, in any sort of benevolent deity, is a disgrace to human dignity and intelligence" (268) but acknowledges its usefulness in the face of evil and waste: "I realized that not wanting to see these things as they are, which most people don't, doesn't necessarily make them completely stupid or insensitive or not frightened of life and death. Christianity's just the thing for people like that. A conspiracy to pretend that God moves in such a mysterious way that asking questions about it is a waste of time and everything's all right really. I joined that conspiracy" (269).

The strong religious interest in this novel is something new for Amis, despite Roger Micheldene's Catholicism in *One Fat Englishman*. Here it is no matter of form or creed or trendy developments in the church, but a serious airing of basic religious questions, including the possibility of belief and the likelihood that God, if He exists, is wicked. Bernard McCabe

argues that "in a sudden shift of focus we are pushed beyond
the here and now to find that the ultimate enemy is God. In
The Anti-Death League God gets the sort of treatment that
Professor Welch gets in *Lucky Jim* . . . a sustained offensive."
John Pazereskis concurs that this is a novel about "a malevo-
lent God." Richard Bradford argues that it is "not, as many
have seen it, a bizarre atheistic polemic. Its broader target is
the human propensity for systematic explanation."[8] Christianity is—like psychoanalysis, like counter-espionage—just such
a systematic attempt at explanation, an attempt Willie Ayscue
has had to abandon.

Moti Naidu's consolation (a rather less systematic explanation and evidently the most useful, as he is the most untrou-
bled man in the book) is that "there are no bad things in the
world. . . . Even what might seem to us most horrible can be
rendered endurable by wisdom" (81) and, specifically to James
Churchill: "Death's nobody's enemy. Your enemy's the same
as everybody else's. Your enemy is fear, plus ill feelings, bad
feelings of all descriptions" (270). And he recommends love.

In fact, each man troubled by death has an antidote:
Hunter's is drinking, Naidu's is transcending the material and
cultivating love for life, Ayscue's is the conspiracy of Christianity and the love of music. Churchill's is his love for Catherine Casement, and, as G. O. Roberts observes, "the power
of love is seen at its most triumphant in Catherine Casement
and James Churchill, for each, by love, rescues the other from
the powerful fear that leads to insanity."[9]

Around them, in addition to the ordinary irrelevant population of a military base or a novel, are three other important

THE 1960s

characters. Lucy, Lady Hazell, is a beautiful, wealthy woman who operates a sort of one-woman brothel near the camp. Her talents are for sexual love; she is generous with it, and her drawing room, where the officers wait their turn to go upstairs with her, is the scene of much of the novel. She is carefully portrayed and, despite her inherent improbability, neither outrageous nor crude as a character. She is intelligent, self-aware, and neither masochistic nor nymphomaniac. She simply likes going to bed with men. There is an element of therapy in her ministrations. She is also Catherine's friend and protector, and James and Catherine, once they fall in love, spend most of their time at Lady Hazell's.

Brian Leonard is a somewhat more complex case. The camp's intelligence officer, whose job is to catch presumed spies, he is foppish, foolish, overly trusting of the wrong people. His psychological approach to counter-espionage, along with his vanity, require that he continually reveal what his mission is, rather than hiding it. His suspicions always fall on the wrong people. Basically good, he is also basically unintelligent, and it is no surprise to find out how wrong he has always been. In the end, he learns that he has been used by British intelligence, that instead of being the pursuer of the spies he was in one sense the bait; in another sense, the unwitting collaborator.

His suspicions eventually lead him to Dr. Best, a psychiatrist at the nearby hospital who has treated both Max Hunter for alcoholism and Catherine Casement for "madness." Best is one of the most extreme of Amis's hostile portraits of psychiatrists. Like Moti Naidu, he believes that the troubles people perceive are not real, but his interpretation is a reductionist, crudely Freudian one. Max Hunter's problem, according to him, is repressed homosexuality. (As almost everyone else knows well, it isn't repressed.) Catherine Casement's problem is that she is really a lesbian. In this way he explains Lucy Hazell's motivation as a "Messalina complex" and suggests that her eroticism actually derives from an underdeveloped libido, though his hypocrisy is shown when he almost rapes Lady Hazell himself, then assigns her discomfort to her own sexual shortcomings (something Roger Micheldene did as well: sexual resistance to *me* equals lesbianism). Best is really one of the worst characters in Amis's fiction, the first of his portraits of harmfully wrong psychiatrists but further disfigured by many another flaw, chiefly cruelty. It is a good touch that he is eventually identified as the Chinese spy, beaten up and arrested, even though, on this charge at least, he is innocent.

These are all character relationships, in which this novel is strong. The plot also involves a healthy dose of mystery and suspense about Project Apollo, what it is and whether it will take place, who the spy is and for whom he is working. It is based on Amis's rather old-fashioned Cold War thinking. Though the weapon of mass destruction is not in fact used against the Communist Chinese, who (according to the plot) are about to invade India, and though some of the characters become distinctly queasy about its use, the novel never seems to turn against mass murder. Dying is bad, unfair, and to be avoided wherever possible; but certain kinds of killing seem to be all right. If the threat of mass killing deters the action which would require the fact of it, so much the better. But in this book the Communist threat is real; there is a real and deadly spy in the camp, and the invasion would have occurred if the British had not outsmarted the Communists. It is a political framework which Amis explained in "Why Lucky Jim Turned Right" and used again in his James Bond adventure, *Colonel Sun*. This all seems a bit quaint now, though. The heart of this very solid novel is in its dedication to the hard questions about death on a personal level, an interest in religion which grows in importance in later novels, and its serious picture of love and the way it changes life.

I Want It Now (1968)

The pattern of Amis's progress in the early 1960s is echoed in his books at the end of the decade. *Take a Girl Like You* (1960), which delved more deeply into the complexities of society and the moral dimensions of love than its predecessors, was followed by *One Fat Englishman* (1963), a lighter novel but one with a very sharp satiric bent. Using the American scene for the first time, this novel had at its center a man who was an unmistakable "shit" and "bastard," whose inability to change those traits led him to calamity and misery, but constituted a sort of dignity at the end. After another deeper, more serious novel, *The Anti-Death League*, Amis turned to two very different books. One of them is *Colonel Sun* (1968), his James Bond book (discussed in chapter 5). The other is *I Want It Now*, which revisits the American scene (this time with a

determined attack on American, particularly Southern, traits).
This book is pointed in its satire of social ills. And most sig-
nificantly, it has as its protagonist another "bastard," Ronnie
Appleyard, a man for whom integrity and sincerity are no
more than poses that play well on television. Like Roger Micheldene, Ronnie sees himself for what he is, but unlike Roger,
he reforms. Roger's continuance in his ways deprives him of
love; love gives Ronnie the impetus he needs to become a better man.

I Want It Now is very much a book of the 1960s—published in the "key year" of 1968, the year of the Tet offensive
in Vietnam, student revolt in France and the U.S., and the
Beatles' *Sergeant Pepper's Lonely Hearts Club Band*—and,
as Malcolm Bradbury writes, in this book Amis turns with
some disquiet from liking it here (values his earlier books had
generally supported) to the problems of "the freer, franker,
and often more frantic liberationist attitudes of the 1960s."[10]
Ronnie Appleyard is the perfect 1960s antihero: a fashionable
media figure, a talk-show host, all style and no content. The
narrator gives his outlines fairly bluntly: "Not that, to be fair
to Ronnie Appleyard a second time, he had the least interest in
power as such. Fame and money, with a giant's helping of sex
thrown in, were all he was after"[11]; "He passed for political,
and Left political, because politics, and Left politics, were the
trend, and therefore the route of advancement" (20); as for
love and marriage, "He had not got a wife because he had not
yet found a sufficiently rich girl of sufficiently powerful family who was willing to marry him" (38).

THE 1960s

The course of his life is changed when he meets a bewildering young woman named Simona (usually called Mona or Simon) Quick, a troubled child of the rich, at a party. Simon disconcerts Ronnie by very quickly assuring him that she is interested in sex with him and not only that, ''I want it now'' (30)—i.e., during a party at the home of one of her mother's friends. Both then and later, back at his flat, Ronnie has little use for Simon, especially after he discovers that, despite her expressed eagerness for sex, she is really frigid and terrified. He is on the point of throwing her out of his life when he discovers that she satisfies the one real requirement he has for a woman: her family is enormously wealthy.

This discovery rapidly changes his ideas about Simon. Soon he has managed to get himself accepted by her mother, not really as an approved suitor (he hasn't the wealth for that) but as someone who can accompany Simon and ''keep her happy.'' This role takes him first to the Greek Isles, among a lot of ghastly rich people, some of them titled, who are friends of Simon's mother and her current husband, Lord ''Chummy'' Baldock. Ronnie's growing feeling for Simon, a complex mixture of genuine attraction, pity, and continuing strong feeling for her money, leads him to denounce Lady Baldock for her cruelty to her daughter, and this leads her in turn to denounce him and expel him from the company.

The next section, called ''Fort Charles,'' finds Ronnie again in the company of the Baldocks, this time in the southern United States (Lady Baldock is an American). He has been invited again because of the use to which he can be put;

Lady Baldock wants to use Ronnie to persuade his friend Bill Hamer, another BBC broadcaster, to put her and some of her rich friends on television. At Fort Charles, Ronnie receives a further course in the awfulness of the very rich, this time mostly Americans, who add to the stupidity, self-absorption, and stinginess he witnessed in Greece, absurd Confederate romanticism and racism. Here he sees Lady Baldock's plan to marry Simon to a horrible figure named Student Mansfield. Student is a loud, braying, obnoxious man with an background of dishonor and known sexual dysfunction; to make such a match for Simon is clear evidence of Lady Baldock's malevolence. When, spurred by these discoveries, Ronnie elopes with Simon, he discovers anew the great, immoral power of great wealth when Chummy uses his influence to bend the laws and corrupt the police and bring her back to her mother.

Two things have been building in the novel so far to change Ronnie Appleyard from the self-regarding, insincere user he has been before into a better man in every way. One is the progressive revelation of how awful rich people are. This set is grasping, competitive, mean-spirited, uninterested in anything beyond themselves unless it is another rich person. The epitome of all these traits is Lady Baldock, who illuminates Simon's own behavior when she cries, "What's happened to my champagne? Why is there always this delay? I want it now" (182–83). Though a rich Greek named Vassilikos and a rich southerner named George Parrot behave better than the average, both helping Ronnie on occasion, even they are largely moved by malice; they are "better" because the object of their malice, Lady Baldock, is the same as the object

THE 1960s

of Ronnie's. That is, they operate on the principle that "The enemy of my enemy is my friend."

The other, more important development is that Ronnie's almost purely mercenary pursuit of Simon Quick has turned gradually into something more unselfish—that is, real love. In their brief escape together, he realizes to his surprise "that nothing he had said to Simon the last five minutes, or indeed the whole evening, had made him feel a shit" (204). This precedes an acknowledgment that he was initially after her for her money but has come to love her for herself. One sign of the change is in Simon's new ability to derive pleasure from sex. Bradbury comments: "Some moral explorations have to be conducted before gratification comes. So, just as *Take a Girl Like You* depends on the principle of procrastinated rape, *I Want It Now* depends on the notion of deferred orgasm."[12] Back in London in the last section of the book, Ronnie analyzes his change even more cogently: "He had begun by using niceness, tenderness, what you will, as a specific aid in the Simon situation, as one of the purest means to an end in all history. And then, frighteningly soon, in fact, unknown to himself, he had started enjoying being nice to Simon, started using tenderness as an end in itself, got hooked on the bloody stuff, in fact" (225). (The sardonic way he thinks about this change, along with the evidence that he can still "use" niceness with perfect calculation with others, redeems him from the unbelievability of a complete moral makeover.)

The climax of the novel occurs on Bill Hamer's television show, where, for hostile reasons of his own, he enlists Ronnie in a discussion of the rich, which includes Vassilokos and

Lady Baldock. Predictably, Ronnie's contribution is a lumi-
nously savage attack on the moral shortcomings of the very
wealthy which has the desired effect on Lady Baldock. As it
becomes personal (she knows of course that his resentment of
her role in his affair with Simon is his chief motive) he declares—on live television—that he wants Simon and would
not touch the Baldock money.

The results of this are interesting. They include the rout
of Lady Baldock, assisted by various of her ''friends'' who
join in the attack; Ronnie's self-satisfaction—his restored
sense of well-being is like that of Jim Dixon when he punches
Bertrand Welch and says what he actually thinks of him—and,
oddly, the restoration of Simon to Ronnie, through the un-
likely fairy-godmotherhood of Chummy Baldock. Chummy,
too, appears to have changed. He began as a caricature of a
shuffling, almost witless, aristocrat, showed evidence of very
shrewd judgment by trying to warn Ronnie off Simon, and
then behaves like a normal chap. That he delivers Simon to
Ronnie is a sign that, stimulated by Ronnie's example, he is
rebelling against his wife slightly; but, on a more cynical level,
it is a sign that, now that Ronnie has renounced any interest in
the family money, Simon is available. She can be permitted to
marry whom she wishes so long as no money is involved.

This novel, then, embodies a sort of reverse Cinderella
plot, making for an interesting contrast with *Lucky Jim*. There,
Jim Dixon was a basically good man stifled by the necessity of
pretending to be something he was not; becoming honest with
the world freed him from restraint and earned him the love of
a good woman and a sharp rise in fortune. Since *Lucky Jim*,

THE 1960s

Amis's fiction has shown a steady progression in the unattractiveness of his "heroes," who have become "less bastard-detectors than bastards themselves."[13] Ronnie Appleyard begins as just such a successful amoral schemer who through love discovers that "I've had to give up trying to be a dedicated, full-time shit. I couldn't make it, hadn't the strength of character" (254). His ethical rise is accompanied by no material improvement, however, instead impairing his prospects of marrying money. Nevertheless, it is curative: he no longer feels like a "shit," Simon's frigidity is well on the way to a cure, and *I Want It Now* provides as nearly unambiguous a happy ending as Amis has given a novel since *Lucky Jim*.

The Green Man (1969)

In his next novel, Amis turned to something very different, a ghost story. Though it is also partly the story of a man learning not to be such a bastard, this reformation is very imperfect, the stimulus for it is much more extreme (ghostly visitations, the near-murder of his daughter by a man dead hundreds of years, a conversation with God), and the interest of the novel is much more distributed beyond the change in the protagonist to the peculiar events which motivate it.

Nevertheless, the central character, Maurice Allington, deserves scrutiny—partly because he is another of a series of Amis men who, though they think they love women, actually don't, men whose love of women really goes no further than enjoying heterosexual sex, wanting it immoderately, and deciding to be as agreeable to women as is necessary to get them into bed. Such men are often very agreeable, very smooth. But the books force their readers to recognize that what these men call their "love" is something else entirely. Amis has drawn portraits of this type in Patrick Standish and Roger Micheldene, and he provides further variations in later novels including *Jake's Thing* and *Stanley and the Women.* Though it has become common to accuse Amis of being a misogynist who fears, hates, and/or does not understand women, it is more just to recognize that he presents such characters in his fiction, and that they eventually are recognized as such, usually by a woman, and their failings accurately diagnosed (e.g., Roger by Helene in *One Fat Englishman,* Patrick by Jenny in *Take a Girl Like You,* though she robs her denunciation of some of its sting by almost immediately taking him back).

Maurice Allington might be thought of as a man in midlife crisis. At age 53, he has a second wife with whom his relations are friendly but remote, a teenaged daughter who hardly speaks to him, a business (running the posh inn The Green Man) that no longer holds his interest. His health is shaky; in addition to (or as a result of) his obvious alcoholism, he suffers from "jactitation," spasmodic jerking of the limbs at night, and hypnagogic hallucinations. He is clearly a mess. In the novel, his father dies. Most of Maurice's attention, until more important things partially intervene, is devoted to seducing Diana Maybury, his doctor's wife, who is also his wife's friend; and then maneuvering Diana and his wife Joyce into bed as a sexual threesome. He succeeds in getting Diana and Joyce into bed, but they shun him and, as the novel ends, are

THE 1960s

leaving together. Joyce tells him, "I don't know what you
think about people, which is bad enough, but you certainly go
on as if they're all in the way. Except for just sex, and that's so
that you can get them out of the way for a bit. Or you just treat
them like bottles of whisky—this one's finished, take it away,
bring me another one."[14] This diagnosis is fairly accurate.

The other trend in Amis's novels that appears here very
strongly is an interest in religion. No one in this book is *religious,* least of all the repulsively trendy Anglican clergyman
who relegates Christian faith to the category of outmoded
nineteenth-century beliefs which also includes evolution. But
the novel is about life after death and the continuation of the
spirit—in the form of ghosts—about supernatural power and
about God. Richard Bradford, believing that this is the novel
"through which the author himself confronts matters of belief
and existence," calls it Amis's "most 'serious' novel."[15]

Allington's inn is "known" to be "haunted" by a certain
Dr. Underhill, a seventeenth-century divine who was suspected of killing two people. Of course, this reputed ghost is
an intriguing feature to draw tourists and entertain diners, until Allington begins to see ghosts. The plot is fearsomely complicated, but includes conversations with Dr. Underhill, whom
Allington discovers to have been an infamous magus who used
his magic to rape teenaged girls. The other branch of his powers was his ability to conjure a gigantic being, made of vege-
tation, that stalked and killed his victims (this is the Green
Man, after whom the inn is named). Underhill appears to
Allington in a tantalizing way, and by digging up his grave
(in company with his mistress Diana), Allington finds other

secrets. Much of his motivation, incidentally, is to prove that he is not mad, as his family suspects, or subject only to alcoholic hallucination.

The oddest part of this novel is the appearance of God, who is described as

> about twenty-eight years old, with a squarish, clean-shaven, humorous, not very trustworthy face, unabundant eyebrows and eyelashes, and good teeth. He wore a dark suit of conventional cut, silver-grey shirt, black knitted silk tie, dark-grey socks and black shoes, well polished. His speech was very fully modulated, like that of a man interested in discourse, and his accent educated, without affectations. Altogether he seemed prosperous, assured and in good physical shape, apart from his pallor. (199)

God chats with Allington for some time, answering questions about the afterlife, about the limits on man's freedom and God's foreknowledge, and so on; but his real purpose is to warn Allington against Underhill.

The climax of the story comes when Allington conjures Underhill, who somehow summons up his Green Man, which assaults Allington's daughter. Throwing a cross at him makes him stop, and a later exorcism, which the infidel vicar conducts against his will and despite his ennui, rids the house and the area of Dr. Underhill.

But what does it all mean, one may be tempted to ask. One answer is that it need not be any more than a thriller predicated on ghostly occupation, with exciting novelties in the form of the Green Man, the visitation of the deity, and the less relevant alcoholism, marital problems, and sex life of Maurice Allington. (The alcoholism is actually not irrelevant; it makes him less likely to be believed when he claims to have seen ghosts.) Amis is on record as thinking highly of fiction that entertains ordinary people by the traditional means of suspense, pacing, and emotional shock.

But there is more to it, or at least the novel seems to ask readers to see more. Maurice Allington is *chosen* to be visited by the supernatural; what does it do to him, what does he learn? The answer to this is somewhat disappointing. Maurice ultimately realizes that he was chosen as a means for Dr. Underhill to get at the teenaged Amy (his specialty was assaulting young girls). In the recent television version of the novel, Maurice has a dream in which his daughter appears to him as a desirable sexual object, and if this is the etiology, then Dr. Underhill's evil is somehow interior to Allington; the Green Man is living out his own unexpressed desires as well as the Doctor's.

But the novel does not seem to encourage such a reading (as Amis's suspicion of Freudianism would lead a reader to expect). It is true that at the end Maurice writes off his marriage with good grace, acknowledging his faultiness as a husband, and that he and his daughter establish closer relations (after all, he has saved her life). None of this has much feeling of inevitability, or closeness to the horrible events that preceded it, and neither does his closing meditation:

> I found I had begun to understand the meaning of the young man's prophecy that I would come to appreciate death and

what it had to offer. Death was my only means of getting away for good from this body and all its pseudo-symptoms of disease and fear, from the constant awareness of this body, from this person, with his ruthlessness and sentimentality and ineffective, insincere, impracticable notions of behaving better, from attending to my own thoughts and from counting in thousands to smother them and from my face in the glass. (252–53)

Following a section that has shown Maurice changing and humanizing, this conclusion, by suggesting that no change is possible this side of death, makes for an odd, frustrating, and even somewhat perverse commentary on the events of the plot. There is no question that Amis means to endow these events with a significance beyond their potential to horrify— to show that Maurice's lechery and selfishness somehow have *brought them on*—but the conclusion tends toward a different meaning. It seems a gloomy reflection added on to suggest that, in some way, all Dr. Underhill's charms and even God's appearance have done little to alter the stubborn Maurice Allington.

Notes

1. Clive James, "Profile 4: Kingsley Amis," *The New Review* 1 (July 1974): 21.

2. Leslie Paul, "The Angry Young Men Revisited," *Kenyon Review* 27 (Spring 1965): 348; Kenneth Hamilton, "Kingsley Amis, Moralist," *Dalhousie Review* 44 (1964): 346; cf. D. R. Wilmes, "When the Curse Begins to

Hurt: Kingsley Amis and Satiric Confrontation," *Studies in Contemporary Satire* 5 (1978): 14–16.

3. James 24.

4. Kingsley Amis, *One Fat Englishman* (New York: Harcourt, Brace & World, 1963) 71. Further references are noted parenthetically in the text.

5. James 24.

6. Dale Salwak, "An Interview with Kingsley Amis," *Contemporary Literature* 16 (1975): 12–13.

7. Kingsley Amis, *The Anti-Death League* (New York: Harcourt, Brace & World, 1966) 193. Further references are noted parenthetically in the text.

8. Bernard McCabe, "Looking for the Simple Life: Kingsley Amis's *The Anti-Death League* (1966)," *Old Lines, New Forces: Essays on the Contemporary British Novel, 1960–1970*, ed. Robert K. Morris (Rutherford: Fairleigh Dickinson University Press, 1976) 68; John Pazereskis, "Kingsley Amis—The Dark Side," *Studies in Contemporary Satire* 4 (1977): 32; Richard Bradford, *Kingsley Amis* (London: Edward Arnold, 1989) 53.

9. G. O. Roberts, "Love and Death in an English Novel: *The Anti-Death League* Investigated," *A Festschrift for Edgar Ronald Seary*, ed. A. A. MacDonald et. al. (St. Johns: Memorial University of Newfoundland, 1975) 212.

10. Malcolm Bradbury, *No, Not Bloomsbury* (New York: Columbia University Press, 1988) 212.

11. Kingsley Amis, *I Want It Now* (New York: Harcourt, Brace & World, 1969) 14. Further references are noted parenthetically in the text.

12. Bradbury 213.

13. Bradbury 213.

14. Kingsley Amis, *The Green Man* (New York: Harcourt, Brace & World, 1970) 244. Further references noted parenthetically in the text.

15. Bradford 59.

CHAPTER FIVE

Genre Fiction and
Short Fiction

$\mathbf{K}$ingsley Amis has always been interested in what is called "genre fiction"—that is, specialized kinds of fiction that can be distinguished from "the mainstream novel" by their own special code of conventions, by their popularity and (usually) lack of artistic pretensions, and by their being generally less respected kinds of writing—for example, mysteries, spy stories, westerns or science fiction. "Genre fiction," then, is usually a pejorative term, used to marginalize certain kinds of writing. Amis has resisted that marginalization, by generous criticism of "genre fiction," including his books on science fiction and James Bond, and by his own practice. John McDermott points out that "it is important to Amis to assert that, without becoming trashy, popular forms of writing are capable of greatness in their own terms and as themselves."[1] Without calling it genre fiction, Amis has given a good definition of what it means, in his foreword to his own *The Crime of the Century:* "The reading on which my writing has been founded was always various, even indiscriminate, including as it did and taking seriously not only 'straight' novels but adventure stories, ghost stories, spy stories, detective stories, science fiction. (I missed the Western, or rather confined my interest in it to the cinema.) By 1975 I had made some sort of contribution to all these genres. . . ."[2]

The Green Man appears in another chapter because it seems to be more than just a ghost story (the ''more than just'' formulation admittedly is itself invidious) but it brings out the fact that the line between ''genre'' fiction and ''mainstream'' fiction is hard to draw. None of the books discussed in this chapter is limited, for its interest, to suspense, novelty, or the ability to arouse dread. And some of the books considered as mainstream include mystery and adventure among their qualities.

Nevertheless, it is possible to make a rough distinction, which is a bit like Graham Greene's division of his books into novels and entertainments. Among the entertainments or genre books here are *Colonel Sun* (1968), which is a James Bond adventure story; *The Riverside Villas Murder* (1973) and *The Crime of the Century* (1989), which are (in a term used in both texts) '' 'tec yarns.'' There is also a touch of the ''police procedural'' in these books, qualified by Amis's own confessed ignorance of what procedure policemen actually follow. *The Alteration* (1976) is a science-fiction novel of a peculiar sort, perhaps better called ''Time Romance'' or ''Counterfeit World''—terms from the book. *Russian Hide-and-Seek* (1980) is subtitled *A Melodrama* and is also a sort of Counterfeit World book. *The Egyptologists* (1965) is harder to classify; a sort of fantasy, it is also a novelty in having been written with Robert Conquest. And Amis's short fiction belongs in this class for two reasons: One is that it is clearly an alternative activity to writing novels, and considered by the author as a lesser one. The other is that many of his stories occupy the same generic niches as these novels—science fiction, mystery, horror, and spy adventure.

The Egyptologists (1965)

Robert Conquest is an old friend of Amis's, an American, a poet and Soviet specialist, and a political thinker of pronounced conservative views. Amis's *Memoirs* contain a chapter detailing their meeting some forty years ago, their various collaborations, Conquest's poetic abilities—best at light verse, Amis believes, particularly in the obscene or scatological vein—and what Amis thinks of Conquest's wife. Their joint activities include being published in the same poetry anthologies, including *The New Oxford Book of Light Verse,* which was edited by Amis himself; editing five science-fiction anthologies, called *Spectrum* I through V (1961–1966); and joint authorship of some political broadsides on educational policy in Britain, three of which are published in *The Amis Collection* as "The Anti-Sex, Croquet-Playing, Statistic-Snubbing, Boyle-Baiting, Black Fascist Paper," "A Short Educational Dictionary," and "ILEA Confidential." All three of these are heavy-handed and bad-tempered where they mean to be delicately funny; whatever their contribution to the argument about the nation's education in the late 1960s and early 1970s, it is hard to see much point to them today.

One of the most sustained Amis/Conquest collaborations, though, produced the novel *The Egyptologists.* In an interview with Dale Salwak, the author explained how he and Conquest wrote the book: "Robert Conquest wrote the original draft which had the idea in it, and most of the characters in it, and a lot of the dialogue, and the science fiction dream, the Nefertiti statue, and so forth. I put in the plot, I introduced the women in fact, and the television debacle."[3]

The Egyptologists is an extremely complicated and highly playful concoction. In chapters prefaced by quotations from *Antony and Cleopatra*, Amis and Conquest depict a group of men who pretend to be Egyptologists as a front for escapist activities motivated by a silly sort of men's liberation theory. Calling themselves "virists," they want to escape from their wives and to free themselves for adulterous affairs, and the Egyptian Society, with its club premises and its pretended lecture every Thursday night, is the ideal cover for them.

The picture of the Society is amusingly done. The members, most of them rather pathetic types, have very elaborate regulations and preparations for breaches of security, emergency plans to handle approaches by people who know or care something about Egyptology, and so on. The plot arises from various threats to their cozy operation. One member has an affair with another's wife; another wife becomes suspicious and begins investigating; someone wants to film a television interview, which would reveal the ignorance of any real Egyptology in the society. At the end, all but three of the members break up the organization, while they race around escaping the police. The "Secretary" of the society is caught just before he can bomb Somerset House (the repository of records of marriages, births, and deaths), in his crazed assault on the institution of marriage.

The farcical events in the plot develop rather inconsistently out of the original premise, which is clever enough, and the plotting, though hectic, seems forced. There is more: not only are the machinations of the "virists" undone, but they are shown as having been, for the most part, not worth the effort. The end, as the imposture of the Egyptologists is discovered, reveals that most of the wives have known the true nature of the group all along but haven't cared, either because they didn't mind their husbands' absence (easy enough to believe) or because they used the cover for their own adulteries.

The virulent hostility to women (or at least to wives) in this book provides an interesting instance of the misogyny that is sometimes a feature in Amis's fiction, and of which he is often accused himself. There is no question that the Egyptologists are misogynists. The only thing that brings them together is a shared distaste for women's company (except for sex) and a dedication to freedom from female control. They indulge in visions of the future in which there are no women, or no marriage.

But is it a misogynist book?—a question that will arise again with *Jake's Thing, Stanley and the Women,* and other Amis productions.[4] On the one hand, it has at its center a group of misogynist men who speak long and loud of their hatred, resentment, and fear of women. The central characters—"heroes" is wrong for this book—feel this way as much as the more marginal obvious eccentrics. So the book is full of misogyny. On the other hand, these are all fictional characters, from whom it is dangerous to infer the views of the author. Just as Shakespeare should not be accused of sharing the

GENRE FICTION AND SHORT FICTION

views of Iago, so, this argument goes, Amis can *create* misogynist characters, invent even fairly loathsome things for them to say, without agreeing with them. Or at least not all the time; asked about the "aggressive attitude towards women and an almost prurient obsession with sex" of the male characters in *Stanley and the Women,* Amis replied "I sometimes think like that. Yes. I think most men do from time to time."[5]

In addition to distinguishing the author from the characters, readers should notice the shape of the novel and how the plot rebukes misogynist attitudes. The characters in *The Egyptologists* receive their comeuppance, as does Roger Micheldene; in other novels, including *Take a Girl Like You* and *Jake's Thing,* the characters whose sexual attitudes are objectionable receive an eloquent denunciation from another (usually female) character. So it is by no means a simple thing to decide if *Amis* is a misogynist on the basis of his frequent use of women-hating male characters in many of his novels; nevertheless, his books sometimes have a tone, or feel, of hostility towards women that cannot always be dismissed by mentally distinguishing Amis from his creations or by noting the details of the plot. It is a problem that affects the understanding of a good bit of Amis's late fiction.

Colonel Sun: A James Bond Adventure (1968)

Ian Fleming, author of the James Bond books, died in 1964. In 1965 Amis published *The James Bond Dossier,* a critical study of Fleming's body of work, which emphasized not only appreciation and praise of the Bond books but also defense of them against various charges of racism, misogyny, sadism, imperialism, and (more subtly) stupidity and unfitness for educated readers. Amis's defense against the first three charges consists of a minutely knowledgeable examination of the books, showing Bond to be more sensitive, tolerant, and so on than less careful readers (probably by this time influenced by the movies) charged. In 1968 Amis, writing under the pseudonym Robert Markham, published his own contribution to the Bond oeuvre.

In it he remains faithful, for the most part, to what readers of the Fleming books would know of Bond. This faithfulness would be important to Amis, who sees the conventions of Fleming's fiction as important, and to Fleming's admirers. To others it may seem perverse, and an Amis admirer, Richard J. Voorhees, writes that "it is slightly depressing to watch him as, knowledgeably and conscientiously, he follows every detail of a drill which was absurd enough in the beginning and has now become a nuisance."[6] Bond is patriotic, resourceful, brave, strong, knowledgeable about many things, attractive to women. The plot, as expected, takes 007 to an exotic location—this time the Greek Isles. Bond's lover and female assistant is called Ariadne and one of the islands is associated with Theseus, so there is a network of allusions that doesn't contribute to the novel greatly, except sometimes by enlightening Bond. The story springs from the kidnapping of M, head of the Secret Service, and what seems to be the attempted kidnapping of Bond at the same time, along with the vicious murder of the servants. Artfully dropped clues lead Bond to

GENRE FICTION AND SHORT FICTION

Greece, where he immediately comes in contact with the Soviet spy network.

Here Amis provides an interesting turn. For one thing, there is no SPECTRE or SMERSH here, just the usual secret services (the hopes of the Western Alliance, touchingly, rest on Britain); the kidnapping is the responsibility of the Chinese, but Bond's presence in Athens involves him with the fairly unperceptive Soviets. He soon makes common cause with the Soviets, chiefly their Greek operative Ariadne, in the desperate effort to stop the Chinese, whose aim is to blow up a secret meeting of Communist delegates being held in (of all places) Greece. This will of course produce consternation among the Soviet bloc, and, because the bodies of Bond and M are to be found nearby, blame for the West.

Naturally, Bond is captured by the villain, the Chinese Colonel Sun; naturally, he is tortured; naturally, he escapes, kills many of the bad men, saves M and Ariadne, and frustrates the apocalyptic plot. This is part of the ironclad convention that Amis has accepted in taking on an 007 novel.

The places where he declines to echo Fleming provide interesting insights into his thinking. One of these is the enemy. In *The Anti-Death League*, published in 1966, the enemy is China, millions of whose soldiers are on the point of invading India until scared off by Project Apollo; here again the evil is Chinese, and the Soviets, though still the other side, behave honorably and cooperate with Bond against Sun.

Perhaps there is some racial reason. The Soviets in *Colonel Sun* are Europeans, men like Bond who pursue a different political end; the Chinese, by contrast, are alien; and their

willingness to kill goes beyond ordinary efficiency into an in-
scrutable ruthlessness. Colonel Sun is evil enough, though
smooth and polite as well; in accordance with the convention
of James Bond books, he is more than eager to explain his
plans to Bond, unaccountably slow (and unreasonably inven-
tive) in killing him. Insofar as he is meant to inspire the sort of
horror of the hardly human that Fleming's villains aspire to,
Colonel Sun is a bit of a flop. He is taller and thinner than the
usual Chinese, and has some other physical oddities, but he is
by no means bizarre enough to compete with Dr. No. This may
be Amis's own realistic credo, his bent toward normality,
counteracting the far-out effects that the Bond books ordinarily demand.

Another example of a correction toward the everyday is
in the complete absence of effective gimmickry in this book.
As usual, Bond visits the armorer who provides him with min-
iature weapons and communication devices. At the end of the
book he realizes that he has never thought of making any use
of them, having relied instead on brains, courage, and British
resourcefulness to block Colonel Sun's plot. This feels like a
good-natured rebuke to the fantastic technology of Fleming's
Bond books.

A less realistic quality appears when Amis provides
Colonel Sun with a companion in evil, a certain von Richter, a
former Nazi and still an active torturer. The point of von Richter may be to provide the *frisson* of pure evil which Colonel
Sun fails to evoke and which is a more automatic response to
the Nazi; in addition, because he was in Greece during the
War and tortured members of the Greek Resistance in a bar-

baric way, he helps to motivate the Greek former partisans, whether Communist or anti-Communist, to oppose Sun and help Bond.

Colonel Sun is, then, a quite satisfactory James Bond book—a bit short on the fantastic elements at which Fleming excelled, because Amis's mind is of a different sort—but with the appropriate elements of violence, sex, suspense, and saving the Empire.

The Riverside Villas Murder (1973)

Amis's next venture in genre fiction is both a murder mystery, with professional detectives and amateur sleuths involved in its solution, and "a fond evocation of childhood."[7] An evocation of childhood may be set in any time, of course, but Amis has set this one at roughly the time of his own childhood, in the 1930s. The result is a host of period details about orchestras on the radio, magazines and serials, the whole densely realized popular culture of middle-class South London suburbia. There is little Depression-era feeling of deprivation; the Furneaux family is a moderately comfortable, two-parent, one-child unit.

As one would expect from a murder mystery, there is a significant period of exposition, in which the author introduces the reader to a half dozen characters, several of whom seem possible candidates for murder and some of whom seem conceivable murderers. A minor crime has been committed—someone has robbed the local museum of some jewels and the

UNDERSTANDING KINGSLEY AMIS

"Longbarrow Man," a skeleton of some historic significance. Then someone is killed. In this case, it is a creepy man named Christopher Inman, who turns up at the Furneaux home when Peter is there alone, fatally wounded in the head and soaking wet from the nearby river. The policemen who have been investigating the museum robbery turn their hands to the murder, and their conversations among themselves (complete with rivalry, class animosity, and the firm conviction by some that others are on a completely wrong track) form much of the rest of the book. There is a skillfully created false lead, as Peter's father has a motive for the murder and no alibi. There is the question of whether the murder of Inman and the theft of Longbarrow Man are somehow related (naturally, they are). There is another attack with a weapon like that found after the murder of Inman.

By these means, Amis raises the suspense level of the novel. His focus on Peter, meanwhile, has several consequences. One is that Peter (who, after all, did discover the first murder) is more and more taken into the confidence of the detectives, particularly a Colonel Manton, and becomes deeply involved in the solution of the crime, including acting as a decoy to bring out the murderer. Another is that (unusual for a detective story, certainly of the 1930s) *The Riverside Villas Murder* contains a good deal of sex. Peter is fourteen, and not surprisingly his mind runs much on sex. One of his friends has supplied him with a Code of Dishonour, a sort of recipe for seduction, which he tries to apply to his neighbor, Daphne Hodgson, with no success. From time to time he visits another friend, Reg, with whom he smokes cigarettes, listens to jazz records, and indulges in mutual masturbation. The town in which Peter lives has a full share of adulterous relations, some well known, and even Colonel Manton turns out to have a homosexual interest in Peter, unpursued and acknowledged wistfully.

But the most important sexual relationship here is between Peter and his neighbor, Mrs. Trevelyan, who appears first as a friendly grown-up, able to talk sensibly with Peter, with an incidental sexual appeal to Peter, of which he assumes she is unaware. Soon she takes an opportunity to show that she is fully aware of it and in fact seduces him in her home at tea-time. This scene is well enough written to obscure part of its unlikelihood and the rather melodramatic way Mrs. Trevelyan turns from passion to accusing herself of being a whore. Peter, naturally, has no complaints and raises few questions, though there is some discussion of Mrs. Trevelyan's fondness for being the dominant partner in sex (which sometimes appears in Amis's fiction as a danger signal for a woman, for instance Simon in *I Want It Now*).

The sexual initiation, the growing responsibility for his family in the absence of first his mother (off on a visit when the murder occurs) and then his father, who is arrested, the mature intelligence he shares with the police, the acceptance of what he learns about his father's feet of clay, and finally his role in the solution of the murder: all these make *The Riverside Villas Murder* a coming-of-age narrative for Peter Furneaux. Peter's early credo—"How nice the nice things in life were, he thought"[8]—when nice things means listening to the radio and reading *The Aeroplane*, gives way to a more complex understanding that nice things can be evil. Meanwhile, the reader discovers who killed Inman, why, and with what—all kept mysterious until the end—and these discoveries are consistent with what has gone before. As in his other ventures into genre fiction, Amis has set himself a set of rules to follow (this may be one of the appeals of writing detective fiction, as it is certainly one of the appeals of reading it) and worked carefully within those rules. Following the rules is not all, and the pleasing portrayal of Peter Furneaux and his sexual development, along with some well-drawn secondary characters, goes beyond the outline, but Amis likes following the rules, as he likes poetry that rhymes and scans.

An unusual feature of this book is that the rules are incorporated into the text, by means of Colonel Manton, who, in addition to being a crack detective and a dormant pederast, is a connoisseur of detective fiction, of which he has a large library. As he says, lending Peter one of his books: "You'll find the blurb, the summary inside the jacket, is rather misleading as regards one crucial point. But I think that's more or less legitimate, don't you? After all, the whole raison d'être of a murder story is to trick the reader. Isn't it?" (160).

Even more obviously an internal aid to the reader is what Peter reads in another book borrowed from Colonel Manton: " . . . When A is murdered, and B and C are under strong suspicion, it is improbable that the innocent-looking D can be guilty. But he is. If G has a perfect alibi, sworn to at every point by every other letter in the alphabet, it is improbable that G can have committed the crime. But he has" (81). This kind of internal commentary on the procedures of the novel is something rare for Amis, whose opposition to many modernist traits usually extends to reflexivity or self-consciousness. But it is a feature of *I Like It Here,* as David Lodge has cogently argued, that connects that novel with Nabokov's *Pale Fire.*[9] And it is even more developed in Amis's next genre novel, *The Crime of the Century.*

The Crime Of The Century (1975)

This is probably the thinnest and least significant of Amis's full-length fictions (the shortest, as well). In it he turns from the one-murder-in-a-small community murder mystery to one involving many murders all over London which announce, in an occult way and for no very good reason, what the final crime will be—the murder of a very august personage indeed. Because of the shocking series of crimes, it is thought best to assemble a sort of blue-ribbon committee to deal with, or at least give the appearance of dealing with, the case; the committee includes members of Parliament, distinguished doctors, lawyers, and psychiatrists, a well-known critic of the ''sick society'' of a vaguely R. D. Laing bent, a successful pop singer, and a crime writer. From the comparison of their deliberations and the crimes as they unfold, it becomes clear that a member of the committee is the murderer. But who?

Most of them are provided with, if not clear motives for killing young women, at least suspicious traits: either they show signs of sexual kinkiness, or they sneak home at night from unknown places for unknown reasons, or they seem bent on proving either that we are all guilty or that some people are guilty and should be executed. An additional ingredient is supplied by the British Liberation Army, a vaguely IRA-like organization, which demands a ransom in return for the cessation of the murders. The solution *is* a solution, though it does not feel particularly inevitable; it would have been no more surprising if one of the other suspects had committed the crime. And this may be because the characterization is so thin. It is almost impossible to remember which character is which, particularly among the police, though Amis has provided each with one identifying characteristic.

Both the thinness of the characters and the mechanical feeling of the plot result from the conditions of publication. For *The Crime of the Century* is a bit of a gimmick. It was published in six weekly installments in the *Sunday Times* during 1975. Designed as a "summer-holiday serial," it clearly was not meant to make many intellectual demands; and, shaped for newspaper publication, it had to be short (as the English summer holiday is really only six weeks long). The demands of serial writing, well known to readers of Dickens and Thackeray, include a climax of sorts in each episode and a mystery at the end to stimulate interest in the next. These demands are met. But the other results of newspaper publication are more unfortunate. In his introduction to the 1989 reprint, Amis comments that space restrictions "meant cutting the whole issue down to the bone, characterisations, descriptions of places and journeys, inner thoughts, any kind of feeling, whatever might be called extra. Well, being forced to drama-

tise absolutely everything must be good discipline for—here
we go again—any kind of novelist''[10]. That must remain matter of opinion. Stripping away inner thoughts and any kind of
feeling robs this book of much that makes Amis's novels moving and interesting.

One more element of trickery is that, after episode five
had appeared in the *Sunday Times*, readers were encouraged to
send in their own episode six, identifying the criminal. The
winning entry was by Howard Martin, and it is printed in the
1989 volume. The two endings, about equally satisfying, both
accord with the facts and finger two different murderers.

The element of self-consciousness that was moderately
visible in *The Riverside Villas Murder* is increased in this book
by the inclusion of Christopher Dane, a crime novelist, as one
of the main characters. In fact, the reader begins reading one
of Dane's own mysteries on page one of this book, and the
effect is like that of a play in which the curtain goes up to reveal actors impersonating people putting on a play. This mo-
mentary confusion has its purpose: the novel Dane is writing
seems somehow to be entangled with the series of murders really happening in London. He becomes a member of the investigating panel and is able to comment on the developing
crime spree as if it were governed by the rules appropriate to
murder mysteries, which, in fact, it is. There are false clues,
obvious suspects who must be innocent, and so on; this inter-
penetration of art and life comes about because the murderer
actually is a " 'tec-yarn" reader. It is an interesting involution
that never quite redeems this novel from being a summer-

holiday serial, quite appropriate for the pages of the *Sunday Times* but looking out of place between covers with Kingsley Amis's name above the title.

The Alteration (1976)

After two murder mysteries, Amis turned to two futuristic novels, both interesting explorations of the form. The first, *The Alteration* (1976), is in fact not futuristic in the ordinary sense, because it is set in the present, specifically in 1976, though a short coda tells of events fifteen years later. Instead, what it describes is a "present" wildly different from the present that is, because it assumes a different past. The key difference is the absence of a Protestant Reformation, and it hinges on a technical change in historical detail—Henry VIII's elder brother lived and had children by Katherine of Aragon. Amis also premises that Martin Luther made an arrangement with the Papacy; instead of leading a schism, he settled for an agreement to alternate the Papacy between Italy and the northern countries, and he is remembered in this book as Germanian I.

This is one alteration: the alteration of history, the creation of an alternative world. *The Alteration* is published in paperback in a series called "Masters of Science Fiction," but science fiction is exactly what it is not, partly because one of Amis's assumptions is that, with continuing Catholic hegemony everywhere, there would be no science. Several of the schoolboys in the book like to read forbidden books, from a category they call Time Romance, one subcategory of which is Counterfeit World. TR (the acronym is used as science fiction readers use "SF") is popular though forbidden. CW is described as "a class of tale set more or less at the present date, but portraying the results of some momentous change in historical fact,"[11] and the boys read a CW book, marvelling at its inventiveness, in which there is no longer any plague, England is schismatic, people fly in airplanes, electricity is used for lighting, Mozart died in 1799, and there is a book called *The Origin of Species.* This is an interesting mirror-like reversal; in a CW tale, the characters read a CW tale which is (nearly, but not quite) the same as twentieth-century, *real* reality.

The alteration of history gives Amis scope for a great deal of invention, both playful and more serious. Among the playful elements are the references to Father Jean-Paul Sartre, to Nazi Heinrich Himmler and Stalinist spymaster Lavrentia Beria as representatives of the Holy Office, to the Brunel spires on the great Catholic cathedral at Coverley (i.e. Cowley, in this world an industrial suburb of Oxford), generally to secular thinkers as good Catholics and secular artists (J. M. W. Turner, Jacob Epstein, David Hockney) as famous for their religious art. The more serious elements of the alteration have to do with the assumptions of what would happen, if Catholic power were unchecked.

The primary effects would be on freedom of thought, which hardly exists in *The Alteration.* As a result, there is no science to speak of and no technology. Air balloons and trains are the latest thing in transportation, while ordinary people ride mules; electricity is known but widely distrusted; plague and consumption are serious threats; Europe is agricultural, not industrial, and the population is, by current standards, small. Moreover, there is no official dissent, though differences of opinion between churchmen and private infidelity exist. And absolute power has corrupted absolutely. The Church does what it wants, including the use of murder against a turbulent priest and the intentional spread of disease as a depopulation measure, the failure of which leads to deliberate losses of millions of men, women, and children in a cynical "Crusade" against the Moslems.

The only exception to the universal sway of absolute Catholic power is in North America, where "New England" is Protestant and roughly coterminous with the original thirteen colonies. There, science is encouraged, democracy of a sort—which does not preclude racism towards Indians and Mexicans—persists, women have more equality with men, and so on; it is altogether a more humane place.

The mainspring of the plot is the almost supernatural singing voice of a ten-year-old boy named Hubert Anvil, a chorister at the English mother cathedral, who is also a talented composer. Hubert sings so well that it is proposed by the churchmen that he be castrated to retain his beautiful soprano voice—the other "alteration" suggested by the title. Hubert, a normal boy who has a normal boy's curiosity about sex, is reluctant to lose this chance, particularly as it is expected to put an end to his composing as well; his father, leagued with all the other authorities around him, encourages him to embrace an opportunity to use his talents for the glorification of God—as well as to be celebrated and even rich.

Hubert Anvil meets the young daughter of the American ambassador and, in effect, falls in love with her; when, in addition, his mother and brother (as well as his more influential fellow choristers) encourage him to rebel, he does so. Entrenched clerical power means that he cannot simply decline, and his family priest, who likewise refuses his assent (mostly because, being flagrantly unchaste himself, he knows what Hubert will give up), is removed from the equation. Hubert's flight involves him in melodramatic adventures, including temporary capture by members of the oppressed Jewish community in London, one of whom recites Shylock's lines from Shakespeare, a writer whose works have been officially banned, though there is mention of a performance of Thomas Kyd's *Hamlet*. He ends by appealing to the only people he knows of who value freedom and oppose papal power, the New Englanders, and is on the verge of making his escape when a sensational turn of events brings him back to captivity, to the hands of the Church, and to alteration.

There are several interesting themes at work in *The Alteration*. One points out how enormous the ramifications of a slight change in historical events can be. Another is that a universal church is dangerous for that very reason; unchecked by protest, the Church has become monstrous. Another explores the dichotomy between perfection of the life or of the work, the traditional challenge for the artist; the perpetuation and perfection of Hubert's life requires that he sacrifice a large and important part of his life. W. Hutchings says that at the center of this book is the "the need to experience the joy of life."[12]

Though this may be broadly true, the most insistent theme is one which is recurrent in Amis: the power of sexual love. The Anvil family confessor, Father Lyall, is asked to give his permission for Hubert's alteration. This is a complex task for several reasons—one, that Father Lyall secretly opposes the operation but his loyalty to Hubert's father means he should defend it; another, his carnal love for Hubert's mother. Hubert's mother, trying unsuccessfully not to be disloyal, explains: "The love we speak of is not the highest but it is the strongest and the most wonderful, and it transforms the soul, and nothing else is like it." (74). Father Lyall himself, formerly only a bad priest, becomes faithless, and tells Mrs. Anvil that he lost his belief because "I found I'd begun to love you as you love me" (128). And Hubert's older brother, a medical student who is dubious about spiritual explanations and transformation, tells him: "I speak of the entirely physical. Or the superphysical: a state of bodily cognisance compared with which all other states are—how can I put it?—unsubstantial and heavisome and bloodless. The man and the woman are so close that nothing else exists for them and they become almost one creature. They're closer to each other than they can ever be to God" (83).

Against this the Church appears as a threat. A New Englander—i.e., Protestant—clergyman offers the explanation that "all their temporal over-magnificence, all their pharisaism, all their equivocation, all their ruthlessness came from one source: the celibacy of their priesthood" (182). This is overstated and at odds with the spirit of the book, which seems more to be claiming that all these things come from the uncontested sway of a Church that has not changed, nor been asked to change, for a thousand years. Its immunity to challenge means that notions like the necessity of celibacy or the superiority of the spiritual over the physical have become lifeless dogmas, nonetheless influential for that.

In a way, this book is a dystopian novel, like Aldous Huxley's *Brave New World* or Margaret Atwood's *The Handmaid's Tale*. By positing a change in the past, it obviates the requirement of placing the negative utopia in the future. On the one hand, it has no point as a cautionary narrative, at least in detail, since the things it would caution its readers against have already failed to happen. On the other hand, if it more essentially depicts a sort of general totalitarian state, with the Church as one form in which it can be realized, then it does have a cautionary point. And the plot follows the fairly conventional plot of the dystopia; in the best-known of these, anyway, there is a rebellion against totalitarian power; the rebellion occurs among individuals motivated by the power of love; and the rebellion fails. All this happens here, and the result is a novel interesting on several levels, from the one on which it is almost a game played by changing history and tracing out its consequences—the level on which people in 1976 are reading Father Bond books—to the highest level on which it speaks profoundly about worldly might, about art, and about the transforming power of love.

Russian Hide-and-Seek (1980)

Russian hide-and-seek is a game in which bored officers go outside at night with pistols, shout, and fire at each other in the dark. It is one of the stays against ennui and meaningless-ness employed by the Russian army occupying England in Amis's 1981 novel, a more conventionally futuristic novel. That is, it is set in the twenty-first century, and, like many such books, depicts a world that is supposed to frighten the reader and to appear a not-implausible extrapolation of current trends. In this case, the extrapolation assumes a conquest of England by the Russians at some point in the second half of this century, followed by a prolonged occupation and a subju-gation of the English to near-servility. As a consequence ma-terial culture has declined (this seems to be a particular Amis worry)—few cars, no televisions, bad food, shoddy clothing, even for the Russian masters, and a nearly medieval level of existence for most of the cowed English population.

How did this happen? It is never thoroughly clear, though one Russian tells another that "there had been disorders here, runaway inflation, mass unemployment, strikes, strike-breaking, rioting, then much fiercer rioting when a leftist fac-tion seized power. It was our country's chance to take what she had always wanted most, more than Germany, far more than the Balkans, more even than America."[13] Thus the "War of Pacification," which despite later propaganda had been very fierce, with many lives (both Russian and English) lost, in-cluding the Queen's.

None of this is of the first importance in *Russian Hide-and-Seek,* which is more concerned with what happens to peo-ple after causes die down. Both the Russian conquerors and the English conquered have become inured to their state. The English rather mechanically call the Russians "shits," and op-

GENRE FICTION AND SHORT FICTION

pose them in petty ways. They have lost their culture, and various attempts in the course of the novel to "return" it to them are almost all failures, including one tragi-comic attempt by the Russians to organize a performance of *Romeo and Juliet* in English, which causes a riot by the English audience, whose members are bewildered by the Shakespeare and end by burning the theater.

More interesting is the psychology of the occupiers, who become the real rebels. Unlike the pattern of most dystopias, in which some of the oppressed, motivated by love, rebel against implacable power, here some of the oppressors, spurred by mixed motives which are partly admirable but also include sheer boredom, try to turn their own power over to their victims. The rebellion in this book, which fails, never enlists English support in any way; instead it is a phenomenon of the younger Russians who see a noble purpose in their quixotic attempt to give the English back, first their culture, then their government.

For here nobody believes in anything. In part, lack of conflict has made people nihilistic and hedonistic. The world is pacified. There are no great causes left, as Jimmy Porter complains in John Osborne's 1956 play *Look Back in Anger* (incidentally, as part of the Festival of English Culture, this play is performed for the English, producing "happy, hearty laughter," from a clearly uncomprehending audience [176]). Perhaps most important, even Marxism is gone. The Russians in this book are more like the officers of *War and Peace* than like the usual idea of twentieth-century Soviets. A colonel explains: "Marxism has ceased to exist. Its followers have died or fallen into cynicism or impotence. And what has replaced it? . . . What has replaced it is nothing, nothingness. No theory of social democracy, or liberalism, anything like that, nor even a non-political code of decency or compassion. And when the computer revolution broke down the idea of progress or just betterment in general broke down too. Christianity had gone long since and none of the new religions and cults took hold'' (98–99). This is what the book is about: spiritual emptiness, moral drift. Despite Colonel Mets's disclaimer, there is a lingering possibility of Christian faith, embodied in an aged cleric who remembers the old days. Alexander, the central character, stands in a church and feels ''there had been something about what had been here, and in innumerable other such places, that men had been ready to die for—long ago, as Mets had said'' (68). Surely, there is an echo of Philip Larkin's poem ''Church Going'' here, the same wistfulness in a secular man for the loss of faith from the world.

A tougher faith is what defeats the rebels; the Security services and the sinister Director Vanag, who prevent the insurrection with contemptuous ease, have something to live by. Vanag explains: ''I realize I'm very lucky, in that I know what to do. I have something to live by—the values and rules of the institution I'm part of and have been part of for many years. Traditions, if you like. Now some of you may argue that those rules and traditions leave a certain amount to be desired, and there may well be something in that. But for me, for us, for these guards, they're better than nothing, which is what you've got'' (224).

Russian Hide-and-Seek is in some part a political fable. Amis's anti-communism, his patriotism, and his feeling that

GENRE FICTION AND SHORT FICTION

England's turmoil promises ill are all obviously working in the creation of this view of the future. There may be a satire on decolonization, too, as the well-meaning but thoughtless young Russians want to turn over rule in England to an English population clearly unfit for self-government and maybe not even interested in having it.

But the book is more obviously about demoralization and the crisis of not believing in anything. Here even love lacks the usual importance Amis gives it. There is plenty of loveless sex (Alexander and an English girl named Kitty, Alexander and a Mrs. Korotchenko) and some sexless love (Alexander's sister Nina and her idealistic fiancé Theodore Markov), but both Alexander and Theodore drift into the "resistance," looking for something they would die for, and they are both destroyed by it.

Short Stories

Kingsley Amis is not one of the important short-story writers of his time. His real field is the novel. In introducing his *Collected Short Stories,* which was published in 1980 and includes almost all his short fiction—sixteen stories—he calls his stories "chips from a novelist's workbench."[14] It seems no injustice to give these chips fairly brief mention.

Most of Amis's best short stories appeared in *My Enemy's Enemy,* in 1962. The good things there are of two sorts: army stories and Wales stories. The army stories, "My Enemy's Enemy," "Court of Inquiry," and "I Spy Strangers," are all set among British soldiers in Europe during the last days of World War II. All of these make some use of the theme of revenge, often along class lines.[15] The fighting has not ended, but they are not involved in it, and the interest in these stories is in their depiction of misfits, men who are not accepted because they are too intellectual, or left-wing, or long-haired, in the mindless world of the military. The depiction of military life, with plentiful supplies of bureaucracy, rank-pulling, and painful boredom, seems accurate, and appears again in books like *The Anti-Death League* and *Russian Hide-and-Seek*. These stories are fully developed accounts of moral crises and moments of revelation—with the compact but powerful effect of the best short stories. They are very fine, especially the complex "My Enemy's Enemy."

The two Welsh stories partake of the atmosphere of *That Uncertain Feeling* and, in their moral squalor, of the poems published as "The Davies Country." In fact the main characters in "Moral Fibre" are John Lewis and his wife Jean, who also appear in *That Uncertain Feeling*. Here an unperceptive, bossy, "helping" middle-class woman tries to force a working-class Welsh woman to behave responsibly, with the opposite result. The conclusion shares with the Army stories the "bolshie" anti-establishment attitude of early Amis: "It was true enough that you had to have social workers, in the same way that you had to have prison warders, local government officials, policemen, military policemen, nurses, parsons, scientists, mental-hospital attendants, politicians and—for the time being anyway, God forgive us all—hangmen. That didn't mean that you had to feel friendly disposed towards any such person . . . " (106–7). All the stories in *My*

GENRE FICTION AND SHORT FICTION

Enemy's Enemy except for "Interesting Things," another Welsh tale, are reprinted in *Collected Short Stories.*

The best of the later collection is "Dear Illusion," in which a poet who has achieved modest success with his work confesses that he only wrote it to make himself feel less awful, that he has always suspected it was no good, and that his latest book proves it. He has written a book of poems as fast as his hand could move, making sure that they vary in treatment but are mostly a bit obscure, and they are celebrated by critics and a prize committee. It is a final joke on them—and on him—and the story seems to make fun of the weaknesses of modern poetry and the herd instinct of critics.

Most of the rest of these stories belong firmly in one or another category of genre fiction. "Something Strange" is a futuristic space-travel yarn, as is "Hemingway in Space"; there are three time-travel stories; "The Darkwater Hall Mystery" is, if not a Sherlock Holmes adventure, at least a Dr. John Watson one, with ratiocination at its heart; "To See the Sun" is an epistolary fiction about vampirism; and "The House on the Headland" shares a setting with *Colonel Sun* but is a mystery about a harem of deformed women.

"Who or What Was It?" is a peculiar tale, apparently narrated *in propria persona* by Kingsley Amis, mentioning his wife by name, the living person Robert Conquest, and other details from the real world. In it he discovers eerie similarities between an inn he visits and "The Green Man," the inn in his novel. This leads on to a ghostly conclusion in which, while Amis walks outside, something in his guise takes his place in the bedroom and, the story concludes, makes love to his wife.

UNDERSTANDING KINGSLEY AMIS

Notes

1. John McDermott, *Kingsley Amis: An English Moralist* (New York: St. Martin's, 1989) 46.

2. Kingsley Amis, *The Crime of the Century* (New York: The Mysterious Press, 1989) vi.

3. Dale Salwak, "An Interview with Kingsley Amis," *Contemporary Literature* 16 (1975): 13.

4. See John McDermott, "Kingsley and the Women," *Critical Quarterly* 27 (Autumn 1985).

5. Val Hennessy, *A Little Light Friction* (London: Futura Publications, 1989) 206.

6. Richard J. Voorhees, "Kingsley Amis: Three Hurrahs and a Reservation," *Queens Quarterly* 74 (Spring 1972): 38.

7. Clive James, "Profile 4: Kingsley Amis," *The New Review* 1 (July 1974): 27.

8. Kingsley Amis, *The Riverside Villas Murder* (New York: Harcourt Brace Jovanovich, 1973) 45. Further references are noted parenthetically in the text.

9. David Lodge, *Language of Fiction* (New York: Columbia University Press, 1966) 261.

10. Amis, *The Crime of the Century* ix.

11. Kingsley Amis, *The Alteration* (New York: Viking Press, 1977) 22. Further references are noted parenthetically in the text.

12. W. Hutchings, "Kingsley Amis's Counterfeit World," *Critical Quarterly* 19 (Summer 1977): 74.

13. Kingsley Amis, *Russian Hide-and-Seek: A Melodrama* (London: Hutchinson, 1980) 230. Further references are noted parenthetically in the text.

14. Kingsley Amis, *Collected Short Stories* (London: Hutchinson, 1980) 10. A subsequent reference is noted parenthetically in the text.

15. Kenneth Hamilton, "Kingsley Amis, Moralist," *Dalhousie Review* 44 (1964): 341.

CHAPTER SIX

Amis in the 1970s

After the 1960s, a very productive and very miscellaneous decade of writing which included four "mainstream novels" as well as the co-authored *Egyptologists,* the James Bond adventure, and a new collection of poems—in addition to university teaching, which he continued until 1963 and resumed briefly at Vanderbilt in 1967—Amis's production remained high in the 1970s, though he sought different directions. *The Riverside Villas Murder* and *The Alteration,* two accomplished genre novels, are of this period. He issued his *Collected Poems,* edited collections of G. K. Chesterton and Tennyson and of essays from *The Spectator* and *The New Statesman,* wrote a short book about Kipling, and edited two very different poetry anthologies. One, *The New Oxford Book of Light Verse* (1978), permitted him to explore a genre of poetry which he sees as undervalued and extremely hard to write well. The other, *The Faber Popular Reciter* (also 1978), was a collection of poems designed to be read aloud or declaimed, and was heavy on sentiment and patriotism. And he picked up the pace of his career as polemicist, issuing public statements on various political, particularly educational, issues.

But the most important development of the 1970s is that in that decade Amis wrote three of his finest novels: *Girl, 20*; *Ending Up*; and *Jake's Thing*. Looked at as a body of work, they illustrate both his particular strengths and his versatility. *Girl, 20* is a study of the trendy personality types (or disorders) which afflicted both the young and the would-be young in the late 1960s and early 1970s. *Ending Up* is something entirely different, a darkly hilarious story of life among septuagenarians. There is no London life; there is no sex; there are no rich people. And in *Jake's Thing* Amis returns to the subject of the baffling nature of personal, especially sexual, relations, as well as returning to the milieu of university teaching for the first time since *Lucky Jim*.

Girl, 20 (1971)

Amis has described more than once how he thought of the idea for this book when he watched a taxi driver pass by a black man who was waiting for a cab, in order to pick up the white Amis. Thinking about this unfairness led him to the character of Sir Roy Vandervane, the central character of *Girl, 20*. Sir Roy is one of the most impressive, most fully rounded characters in Amis's fiction for many years. He is complex, an exasperating but ingratiating figure. A trendy poseur in most ways, he also pitilessly skewers trendy poses in others, as when he pretends to believe that a man wearing dark glasses in London must be blind, hauling him across the street against his protests. In *Girl, 20* Amis has created a full cast of complicated characters, some of them "awful" in the traditional Amis way, some of them "shits" as fully deserving of that name as any psychiatrist in his fiction. But the awful characters are also appealing, and all but one of the "shits" have something to be said for them as well.

It is an odd mixture, this book, a sharp, hilaricus satire on almost everything that an aging and fairly traditional author might associate with "the Sixties"—a period which, as has been noted before, reached its full flower in the early 1970s; which, nonetheless, qualifies all this by a humorous sympathy for all but the worst sufferers from the Sixties syndrome, and a forceful awareness of how limited is the apparent spokesman for Amis's own disapprovals.

The satire on the Sixties follows lines predictable from Amis's journalism, or from simply thinking back on that period and the reaction the older generation had toward "youth" and its excesses. Amis is on record, for instance, in opposition to sexual frankness beyond a certain modest degree, against rock and roll music, against extremes of dress, against left-wing politics, against permissiveness in education and child-rearing, against unclear, sentimentalized attitudinizing. All of these traits are clearly visible in the targets in *Girl, 20*. The chief targets are Roy Vandervane and his wife Kitty, who, though not young (Roy is in his middle fifties; Kitty, his second wife, a little younger), have accepted most of the fashionable ideas of the Sixties.

Their son Ashley, for instance, receives no discipline whatever, and consequently is a monster. When Kitty despairingly asks Roy to use his paternal authority to make him stop indiscriminate peeing in the house, Roy replies: "How? What authority? We agreed he's not to be punished and we can't go back on that."[1] This conversation, as it happens, takes place in a study decorated with "framed posters of Che Guevara, Ho Chi Minh, a nude couple making love and other key figures of the time" (48). This "open" or "free" parenting really amounts to selfish neglect. Ashley is growing up without any guidance, and Roy's grown daughter from his first marriage is a lost soul, knowing nothing, caring for nothing; though she has musical talent, her parents never help her to develop it. At the end of the novel she has become a heroin user.

There are other trendy period traits. Sir Roy has changed his mode of dress, and become "a bulky figure in a wide-lapelled double-breasted jacket that, after a then recent fashion, set up uneasiness in the beholder by looking very, very nearly as much like a short overcoat, a glistening two-tone shirt and hairy trousers with widely separated stripes on them [and with a] rough bob in which his thick, dark, ungreying hair had been done" (33). The Vandervanes have a lodger/chauffeur named Gilbert, a black man who is also their daughter's lover; his main function seems to be to denounce whites and members of the middle class.

The chief arena of interest for Amis in this book is sexual. The title refers to the sexual attractions of younger women (a middle-aged friend has confessed to receiving a thrill just from reading the phrase "Girl, 20" in a classified advertisement). Sir Roy Vandervane, who has had extramarital affairs before, including with Kitty during his first marriage, has begun another one, with a teenager named Sylvia. Douglas Yandell, a friend of the family's, is called in by Kitty to help her sort this one out. It is worse than the average, both because Roy seems more open about it and more committed to Sylvia—this worries Kitty—and—what worries Douglas more—because Sylvia is so awful.

As a representative of youth, she is a damning picture: ignorant and self-indulgent, heartless, rude, given to making scenes, denunciatory of anyone different, self-satisfied, indifferent to the needs of anyone besides herself. Sir Roy recognizes some of this. Douglas Yandell and his own, not-so-young, not-very-glamorous girlfriend Vivienne recognize all of it, but are helpless to do anything to "save" Sir Roy, who is happy to be lost. Sylvia has the indispensable attraction: sexual availability, including willingness to do kinky things, and a youthful body.

His attraction to Sylvia makes Sir Roy begin to think of himself as an honorary young person, and in this role he provides a number of fairly implausible paeans to the young: for instance, "the young deserve a bit of special tolerance and understanding, because they're young and in conflict and have this different vision" (46); later, just before Roy delivers a canting exposition of the difference between "have people" and "be people"—i.e., old and young—he nods his approval while his girl Sylvia explains: "We're not like that. We're different. . . . Uhbsolutely different. We reject money and making your way in the world and setting yourself up in life and rules. All the things they want us to use up our energies on so they can stay in power" (65).

Sir Roy is clearly something of a hypocrite, since he still has plenty of money and belongs to exclusive London clubs and, in general, has already made his way in the world, as his knighthood attests; but he never claims purity of motives. He is required to defend his decision to compose an awful *avant-garde* piece called *Elevations 9*, to be performed with a rock band called Pigs Out for a youth audience; when Douglas Yandell, who admires Roy as a musician, accuses him of a plan to "arse-creep youth," he concedes that he is doing just that, because "there are things I can get from youth I can't get anywhere else" (140). These things, in addition to sex with a young person and the supposedly more virtuous attitudes of the young toward getting and spending, include uncritical admiration.

A striking feature of *Girl, 20* is that, though Sir Roy consists of affectations and pretenses, and though the person for whose benefit most of the affectations are adopted is repulsive, he redeems himself through a deeper honesty, good humor, and the fact that he is still a man of genuine accomplishments, mostly musical. It helps that *Elevations, 9* is a complete flop, leading to Sir Roy being assaulted and his Stradivarius smashed.

That Sir Roy embodies so many of the attitudes of the Sixties that Amis clearly sees as false and even dangerous, and yet is something much more than a mere butt of satire, is partly due to the subtlety and complexity of the characterization in this novel. Sylvia is hardly subtle; she is uncomplicatedly awful. But Douglas Yandell is a different matter. The narrator and an incisive commentator on the foibles of the

AMIS IN THE 1970s

Vandervanes and Sylvia and the "youth scene" generally, Douglas is himself a musician and a music writer; he, too, is interested in sex but has a cozy arrangement with Vivienne, whom he shares with another chap and to whom he has no particular commitment. Douglas is traditional—that is, suspicious of much that is new and of anything that is supposed to be good *just because it is new.* He is witty. Though he fights against a block-headed newspaper editor who resists giving a good review to a performer from a Communist country (and who turns out to be Sylvia's father and an implacable enemy of Sir Roy Vandervane's), he is really unpolitical. Challenged by the West Indian Gilbert, whose provocative conversational gambit is to call him "an imperialist racist fascist," Douglas replies that "the great issue of my time is me and my interests, chiefly musical" (19).

In the hyper-politicized climate of Gilbert and the Vandervanes, this sounds like a common-sense stance, and in general Douglas is the voice of reason and restraint against the excesses of the youth and those who would "arse-creep" them. But this tolerance becomes more troubling in other parts of his life. Towards the end of this novel, Vivienne Copes, the woman in Douglas's life, takes him to meet her father. Questioned by Mr. Copes, Douglas tells him: "I just lead my life from day to day, like most people, whatever they may say to themselves or one another about it—in fact like everybody I've ever met or heard of, apart from a few prophets and such. Which suggests to me that what you say to yourself and your friends about what you're doing can't be very important" (208–9).

Both Vivienne and Mr. Copes argue that you have to believe in something; this conversation ends inconclusively. In the welter of events that climax the book, especially the premiere of *Elevations 9* and the beating of Sir Roy, Douglas thinks little about Vivienne, so he is surprised when she tells him that she is marrying Gilbert and further makes it clear that she chose Gilbert because he believes in something. One sign of this is his insistence on changing Vivienne's style of dressing, which Douglas has always disliked but, tolerantly, said nothing about.

When he tells Vivienne that he disapproves of people trying to stop others from doing what they want (an oddly Sixties-style credo for the traditionalist Yandell) she insists that when you really care for someone else "you've got to really do something about it, take it on. . . . " (249) The novel has arrived, by this point, at an interesting place in the relations of these characters; Sir Roy has made a fool of himself in various ways, but he is going on—on with Sylvia, on with his mock-rock compositions, on with Youth. And even though he is wrong, at least he is committed. Douglas Yandell is neither hot nor cold, and Vivienne finally rejects him. Witty and engaging as he is, agreeable as he is to Amis's own political and social views, Douglas is something of a hollow man.[2] He finds this out in that most typical of scenes from an Amis novel, a scene in which a woman points out to a hitherto complacent man how he falls short of full humanity, the chief example being his failure to treat a woman with human concern. This notification also makes him realize that all his other efforts to "help" have come to nothing, Roy and Sylvia being driven

closer together and Penny now not just idle and unhappy but
on heroin—or, as she puts it, in the chilling last sentence of
the novel: "We're all free now" (253).

Girl, 20 is a major Amis novel, though, not just in com-
bining an important moral stance with its satire on the Sixties,
but also in its comedy. The events of the story, including some
of Sylvia's behavior and Sir Roy's ebullience, are funny; but,
as in *Lucky Jim*, much of the comedy comes from the language
of the narration, particularly its surprising and witty charac-
terizations and similes. For instance, when Penny describes
her own plight in the Vandervane home, Douglas says that
"she might have been a television story editor in conference,
briskly outlining in the first person a substantial minor character she was proposing to have written into the script" (97).
Introduced to two university students, Douglas "battled to
keep out of my voice the senile tremolo I imagined the pair
were willing me to put into it" (20); when Sir Roy pretends not
to have heard what she has said, his wife repeats it:
" '*How* . . . did you *get* . . . *here* . . . from the *station*.' This
came out in chewy, easy-to-lip-read chunks, with churchyard-
pigeon head-effects" (34).

One final source of repeated humor is Sir Roy's vocal
affectation; though well educated and middle class, he has
begun to slur his speech, presumably to "arse-creep" youth
or the working class. There are many examples of this trait,
including "exiss" for "exist," "moce" for "most," and
this early example: "Spot of corm beef'll do me fine. And
some tim pineapple or tim peaches to follow, if they're there"
(35). That Sir Roy talks this way is, of course, a sign of his

willingness to change himself fundamentally, to violate what
his convictions actually are. It is also amusing for readers and
Amis clearly has enjoyed multiplying instances of it, in a way
reminiscent of Bertrand Welch's "you sam" and variants
thereon, in *Lucky Jim*. Sir Roy has another speech habit, that
of substituting clichés, or at least orotund phrases, for obscenity. He does this inconsistently, since he also uses obscenity,
but it seems to be a holdover from a primmer past, and when
really angry he is likely to cry out "School of thought!" or
"Oh, Puck-like theme!" Unlike the deliberate slurring of pronunciation, which expresses solidarity with groups he envies
(youth, the poor, anyone who behaves "naturally"), his use of
euphemisms illustrates nothing about his convictions. It seems
to be included both as another means of rounding the character
of Sir Roy and as a result of the exuberance which makes *Girl,
20* one of Amis's most accomplished books.

Ending Up (1973)

Girl, 20 is set among the young, in the city, in a pros-
perous and artistic milieu, and it contains a lot of sex. In his
next mainstream novel, *Ending Up*, Amis turned to something
completely different. Here a group of sexless oldsters share ac-
commodations at a shabby cottage in the middle of nowhere,
suffering material and spiritual privation. By contrast with the
high spirits of *Girl, 20*, the new novel is quite bleak. The old
people are lonely and unhappy. They scheme against each
other in petty ways; two of them are motivated by snobbery

and malice, while the three who are capable of more generous impulses are handicapped by alcoholism, nominal aphasia and other after-effects of a stroke, and a condition of ugliness and awkwardness which rules out being loved. At the end they all die, some horribly.

This sounds like an unpromising mixture. That it makes a strong and telling and even funny novel is surprising, but it may be partly attributable to the genesis of the novel, which Amis explains as a case of projecting into old age the lives of himself and some family and friends who were then living in a sort of communal household in the north London suburbs. He explains: "The starting point is so often: What would happen if . . . ? In this case, What would it be like if we were all old and all, or some of us, handicapped to some degree? It was a kind of purposeful exaggeration of what is only slightly present or potentially present in existing circumstances."[3] Amis's seeing himself and his friends and relatives in the lineaments of these shattered old people may help to explain why, despite their plight, and despite the "awfulness" of some of them, Amis permits us to read them all from the inside, with some sympathy in every case.

Amis's novels (like most novels, perhaps) can usually be seen as either focalized on or through one character (e.g., *Lucky Jim, That Uncertain Feeling, One Fat Englishman, Girl, 20*) or something more like ensemble works, even if some characters necessarily occupy more of the spotlight (*The Egyptologists, The Anti-Death League*). This one is an ensemble book. Though one person, Bernard Bastable, seems somehow to claim the role of "main character," this is more because of the pungency of his personality and the effect he has on other people than because he is more important, or occupies more of the canvas, or owns the mind through which the narration is filtered. In fact Amis provides inside views of all the characters, major and minor, and the counterpoint among the five old people is quite dexterous.

The inhabitants of Tuppenny-hapenny Cottage are: Bernard Bastable, a bitter man who has been a failure as an officer and a husband and who occupies his time by using his sarcastic wit to hurt those with whom he shares his life; his sister Adela, who is a genuinely good woman but who, despite her desire to give her love to someone, has never even been *liked* before "as the result of her extreme ugliness"[4]; Derrick Shortell, known as Shorty, who was Bernard's servant in the Army, as well as his sex partner, and who serves this household as servant, despite his financial independence, because he is working-class; George Zeyer, a retired professor, a Czech, the brother of Bernard's ex-wife, and a stroke victim, immobile and brain-damaged; and Marigold Pyke, an affected old snob, childhood friend of Adela, enemy to Bernard on grounds of personality and to Shorty on grounds of class.

The novel is structured as a series of set-pieces. Nothing much happens in the lives of these people, limited as they are by illness and poverty and shortage of friends and family. Thus they are in action mostly when someone comes to the house. During a period of a few months in late fall and winter, Tuppenny-hapenny Cottage is penetrated by Dr. Mainwaring, the general practitioner who treats all the inhabitants, on two occasions and by Marigold's grandchildren on two occasions; in addition, Adela leaves the house on errands (she does the shopping for everyone) and Bernard goes to London for a medical examination.

The visits by younger people provide a glimpse of how these old people look to the young. They are very exasperating, and Marigold's grandchildren come only out of obligation, get drunk if possible, and swear never to come again. Keith, the husband of Marigold's granddaughter, "was seized by boredom—a poor word for the consuming, majestic sensation that engulfed him, comparable in intensity to a once-in-a-lifetime musical experience, or what would be felt by the average passenger in a car driven by a drunk man late for an appointment . . . the fellow who coined "bored to tears" would have made a fortune in the slogan-writing game . . . " (128–29). The doctor, likewise a younger man with a more interesting life, finds them all exasperating: confronted with Marigold's annoying slang ("sweetle-peetles" for sweet, "blackle-packles" for black people, "tunkalunks" for thank you), he "only just managed not to scream or to pitch forward on to the tasteful orange-and-buff carpet (once an ornament of her home in Beauchamp Place)" (78).

The double vision, from inside the bonds of age and outside it, permits readers to share the perceptions of the younger visitors—these people are boring and annoying, without being in any way charming in return—while retaining an interest in the old people's situation, views, and fate. It is a feat for a novelist to create a houseful of boring people without boring the reader, to render an existence in which almost nothing happens without turning the novel into the same sort of experience, and Amis has met this challenge very successfully.

The plot, on a local level, is made up of the strategems of the five old people to help time pass. Marigold has the most "resources"; she has memories of an allegedly posh background when she lived in Beauchamp Place, London, and she has two married grandchildren who visit, along with their children. She spends much of her time writing letters and putting on grand airs. George Zeyer has the fewest resources, though he is an intellectual and the most humanely normal of the group; but his stroke-caused immobility is lessened when it is discovered that he can be carried downstairs, and by practice (and very annoying practice it is, consisting of reciting all the nouns he can think of) he overcomes his nominal aphasia. He aspires to return to scholarly activity, though without any real prospects. Marigold has a cat; George, a dog.

The kind and self-sacrificing Adela is responsible, with Shorty's help, for all the cooking, cleaning, and other work around the house. Rather as one would expect, they not only receive little gratitude for their services, but are despised by Bernard and Marigold. Shorty is a simple character, not stupid, willing to suppress himself in order to keep others happy, able to see the other point of view. His pleasures are easily summed up—"This was the squaddie's literal seventh heaven: he was dry, warm, indoors, off duty, smoking, pissed [that is, drunk], and getting more pissed still" (71–72)—but they are also harmless.

Bernard Bastable is the most interesting character, partly because he is the most malicious. A man disappointed in his career, in marriage, in every way, he finds his only satisfaction in making malicious remarks and hurting the feelings of others. Because she is the easiest target, though the least deserving, he hurts Adela the most. He specializes in a superciliousness about pronunciation and lucidity, often achieved by pretending not to understand Adela. As the two strongest characters, who are also in some sense competitors for the attention of Adela and almost completely self-absorbed, Bernard and Marigold are the major antagonists.

Much of the novel demonstrates the strength and childishness of this antagonism. Bernard pretends to forget to bring Marigold a drink she has persuaded him to mix. Marigold speaks woundingly to Shorty and once nearly pushes him into the fire, after he has deliberately spilled wine on her dress. The old are rendered without sentimentality. Though Adela would seem the most obvious focus of any sentimental feelings, even the best-disposed people in the book cannot really like her. The others all lack the virtues age is supposed to bring—wisdom, serenity, acceptance of life—and Bernard and Marigold have become childish in their hatred and selfishness while retaining an adult's ability to scheme and deceive.

The plot consists of slight changes in the characters, or rather proposed changes that fail to occur. Marigold, beginning to become senile, thinks of leaving but decides not to; George improves his memory, plans to become an active scholar again, and fails; and, most importantly, Bernard learns that he is dying, decides to be kind to people for a change, and realizes that he cannot. He has already recognized in himself traces of "the habit of wanting to be mistaken for a man of ordinary decent feeling" (48); under the death sentence of his London doctor, he tries to develop some ordinary decent feeling, or at least fake it, but ends by becoming more hateful than ever. He begins to target the others with puerile tricks—an attempt to make Shorty believe he has become incontinent, a stink bomb in the bathroom designed to shame Marigold, tricks on the dog and cat—which almost all backfire.

The cataclysmic ending, in which Amis renders in cool understated prose the deaths of the five, comes about by accident, though traits seen before—Shorty's carelessness and drunkenness, Marigold's selfishness and malice, Bernard's overly complicated scheming, and even Adela's selfless concern for others—help to explain the accidents.

Michael Barber, interviewing Amis in the *Paris Review,* called *Ending Up* "very bleak," and in very obvious ways it is.[5] It has a disturbing punch. D. R. Wilmes has attempted to explain its complex satiric effects:

> *Ending Up,* with the essential unfairness of satire, assures that the reader will fail [in compassion or "goodness"]. We could say that the satiric target of the book is modern society's attitude toward the aged, its condemnation of them to the roles of the senile and the childish. But the solution is unsatisfying. We've been made to laugh, then made to realize that we've laughed with and at the dragon, who really isn't very funny. In this latest formulation of Amis's art, the curse is directed at us, and it hurts.[6]

This asks the novel to be more didactic than it really is; for instance, modern society has not asked Marigold to be senile or Bernard to be childish—they just are. Modern society, if the younger people in the novel are fair representatives, would far prefer the elderly without the sinister and unappealing traits of age. But they aren't available in a more attractive version. That is the grim truth.

There *is* a dark comedy to this book that qualifies the bleakness. Amis enjoys Bernard, and spiteful as he is, readers can, too. Shorty is a rich and original creation. Adela is a subtle combination of the pathetic and the exasperating. The book is funny, and the humor is not all bitter; much of it comes from seeing the comic side of essentially human traits that are no less human and no less funny simply because their possessors are old people much closer to death than they or readers realize.

Jake's Thing (1978)

In 1978 Amis returned to the milieu of his first novel, the university; *Jake's Thing* also has psychiatry as an important element and psychiatrists as important villains (as in *The Anti-Death League* and *Stanley and the Women*, which was to appear in 1984). And, as in very many of his books, sexual relations are at the heart of the novel. The difference here is that sexual indifference, manifested as impotence, is the important given; Jake's "thing"—in the 1960s usage of his fixation or his specialty—is that his "thing" no longer functions. His impotence goes beyond the bedroom, though that is the only sort he clearly recognizes and the problem that leads him to seek help. Jake is also intellectually limp and futilely angry at the way of the world. Readers have taken their reaction to *Jake's Thing* as telling them something about the mood in which the author wrote it. For instance, Malcolm Bradbury declares that it is "a tale of fundamental sexual manipulations and exploitations, written in what seems a masochistic rage," and Philip Gardner finds that it "gives the impression of a release of control, a relaxation into resentful realism, welcome no doubt to its author but resulting in a book which is too confused and sprawling to make a really powerful impact."[7]

Perhaps the most significant fact about this book, viewed as a stage in Amis's career, is its placing a character who does not like women at the fore, backed by quite a few others who arguably are different illustrations of the same trait. Jake comes to the point of acknowledging that "I don't even like them much. Women. I despise them intellectually. . . . "[8] His homosexual friend encourages him to "go on about not liking women." And he does.

Does *Amis* go on about not liking women? Or does he create male characters who do so and who, regularly enough, are shown up as wrong? In this book, sure enough, there is the moment when Jake is enlightened, or denounced, by his wife, who believes he doesn't like women; later, a lover tells him the same thing; and when, finally, his wife leaves him he decides *not* to pursue any therapy which would restore his libido. Asked to take part in his college's debate over the admission of female undergraduates, he loses his composure and begins to put the case opposite to the one he is supposedly making, urging with great force the argument *against* the admission of women. Clearly Jake has a thing about (against) women. But whose thing is it? Just his, or his creator's as well? This question becomes even more nagging in *Stanley and the Women*.

One of the differences between this novel and *Lucky Jim* and the others of the 1950s and 1960s is that it is about middle-aged people, perhaps with a carry-over from *Ending Up*. Jake Richardson (the name seems to echo Jim Dixon—i.e., Dick's son) has middle-aged worries about his health, the value of his property, the adequacy of his income, the loss of his virility. His loss of energy is not just sexual. He dislikes going out or doing anything, preferring instead to sit in his living room and watch undemanding television shows. Though the novel shows that he was at one time a serious historian of ancient Greece, he is beyond all that now. When finally he returns to Oxford (he commutes from London, spending as little time at the university as possible), his sour reflections take in much of the life around him, including his own intellectual work. His train fills up "with younger persons for the most part, undergraduates, junior dons, petty criminals" (90). He reflects on his lectures and seminar material, not revisited for five years, on a deferred article, on his books of solid scholarship long in the past: "Three or, in the eye of charity, four books were probably enough to justify Dr. Jacques ('Jake') Richardson's life. They were bloody well going to have to" (92). Thinking on these matters, and on the necking of younger passengers in the train, Jake realizes that his indifference betokens no benevolence; instead, "it just went to show how far past caring he'd got" (93).

The main skein of the plot is Jake's impotence and his efforts to cure it. As is usual with Amis, the novel begins *in medias res,* with an unidentified voice asking, ''When did you first notice something was wrong?'' (1). This is Jake being questioned by his general practitioner, who will soon send him on to specialists (that is, psychiatrists) to be cured of his sexual dysfunction. His course of treatment seems designed to humiliate him; he is required to put on a ''nocturnal mensurator'' which records whether he has erections while asleep. Having been asked repeatedly whether he has any objections to displaying his genitals in public, he is forced to do so, in a sort of operating theatre before numerous students. He is made to look at pornography which he does not enjoy and to write down sexual fantasies, the more lurid the better. Having none, he has to make them up, and in this, as in other ways, he disappoints his therapist.

The therapy is disturbing to Jake in two ways. One is that it seems to do him no good, but beyond that, it seems stupid. He has no confidence in the therapist, even in theory, and the facts disappoint him further. This person, Proinsias Rosenberg, appears to be ''a boy of about seventeen'' and ''about two foot high'' (28–29). Worse, he is grotesquely ignorant, unaware that Freud lived in Vienna, that there were revolutions in 1848, or what haggis, the *Titanic,* Herodotus, Van Gogh, the Taj Mahal, or Hadrian's Wall might be. In another way that he never quite realizes, Jake doesn't really want to be cured. His wife Brenda apparently recognizes that his criticism of the process is really a lack of interest in its objective. While attacking the absurdities of his therapy (and they are absurd), Jake seems more deeply unsure whether he actually wants it to succeed.

AMIS IN THE 1970s

The absurdity of the therapy escalates; beginning with experiments in nocturnal measurement and in role-playing (nongenital) sex acts with his wife, continuing through a public demonstration of his impotence, naked, in front of strangers, it leads up to a workshop, and, as Jake says, "if there's one word that sums up everything that's gone wrong since the War, it's Workshop. After Youth, that is" (140). This workshop is of the classic 1970s sort: getting your feelings out, especially if they are violent or embarrassing, in front of other people, and under the scourge of a forceful, nearly fascist, American facilitator. In addition to bullying the participants into tears or other breakdown, there are touching exercises and staring at each other. Predictably, the workshop does Jake no good. Jake has thought earlier, in anticipating his exposure of his genitals to strangers, that it "was just part of the steady progress towards more sophisticated awareness which had come to fuck up (so it seemed to him) most kinds of human behaviour in the last however many years it was" (63). The workshop is a particularly excessive, perhaps even sadistic, kind of openness.

That Jake's impotence resists all psychoanalytic attempts at a cure—in fact, he finally discovers that it is physiological and probably curable with medication—is predictable throughout the book. What sustains the plot is the lengths to which modern "science" is likely to put the emotionally troubled, and the strains on Jake's marriage. Readers of Amis's earlier books will recognize the moment when Brenda, hitherto stolid and relatively uncomplaining, fills in the misguided man on his shortcomings. The shortcomings are real, and the reader is always well ahead of the character who is put right on them. (Similar scenes occur between Jenny and Patrick in *Take a Girl Like You*, Jean and John in *That Uncertain Feeling*, Helene and Roger in *One Fat Englishman*, Vivienne and Douglas in *Girl, 20,* and elsewhere).

The analysis is that Jake is indifferent to Brenda except as sexual partner, that he cares too little to show her any affection or share conversation with her, and that he actually doesn't care about women. Eve Greenstreet, an old flame with whom Jake has a one-night stand, seconds Brenda on this diagnosis.

As far as a reader can determine this seems broadly true. Jake acknowledges it, going so far as to call himself a male chauvinist pig and admit he doesn't like women. His bill of particulars, which he develops at length and with passion before his college's governing body, sitting to consider the admission of women as students, is largely intellectual: "They don't mean what they say, they don't use language for discourse but for extending their personality, they take all disagreement as opposition, yes they do, even the brightest of them, and that's the end of the search for truth which is what the whole thing's supposed to be about" (201–2).

The ambivalence of the reader at a point like this pivots on whether Jake's complaints are the outcries of a male chauvinist pig spurned by wife and lover and almost dead sexually, or an overstated case that nevertheless is supposed to be a sound one. Amis has said that he writes books about good and bad people. Is it bad of Jake to denounce women, their intellects and conversational abilities, in this fashion?[9] The novel provides no good countervailing argument, as Jake's listeners tend to agree with him (admittedly these are cloistered dons, some homosexual) and the argument at the Governing Body is oddly one-sided; Jake, after all, is deputed to argue the case for the admission of women, so someone else argues against it; then, under questioning, he breaks down and argues against it, too.[10]

Despite the troubling way it treats its war-between-the-sexes theme, *Jake's Thing* has several strong non-structural features, including a full panoply of rich characters. There are the people who attend the workshop, an array of unhappy patients; the facilitator, Ed, and even more the psychiatrist Dr. Rosenberg; the other dons at Comyns College; and a disturbed girl, Kelly, who meets the Richardsons at the workshop and pursues Jake to Oxford.

One purely comic creation exploits Amis's mimicry and talent for comic dialogue. The college's head porter, Ernie, serves mainly to josh Jake about his supposedly hyperkinetic sex life and is distinguished by his accent, which Amis specifies as Oxfordshire. It takes the form of exchanging the vowel sound of "bound" with that of "baned." When he really gets going, Ernie comes out with things like "had a night on the tain have you sir? . . . Yes, you always were a bit of a night-ale, like, but never much of a . . . If I didn't know you better I'd have said you'd been draining your sorrows" (192).

The most important characters, largely comic, are Alcestis and Geoffrey Mabbott, friends of Brenda's. Alcestis is a gruff, talkative woman whom Jake thinks of as a World War II vintage officer, nicknamed (by Jake) "Smudger." Her husband Geoffrey is distinguished by peculiar clothes, boringness, and a set of puzzling prejudices Jake calls "the inverted pyramid of piss'' (14). Geoffrey later turns up in the workshop with Jake and Brenda, seeking treatment because, as Ed brusquely explains, he "gets worried because he's figured out he's an asshole'' (150).

Brenda's announcement that she is leaving Jake for Geoffrey is, again, a sort of narrative motif that Amis has used before, like Helen's going off with Irving Macher in *One Fat Englishman* or Vivienne becoming engaged to Gilbert in *Girl, 20*. That is, it provides a judgment on the main male character, who has already been shown to be unaware of, and indifferent to, the woman's real nature and needs. When she leaves him for the man he despises most, it provides a salutary shock (and this may be part of the motivation) and it provides a gauge of how wrongly he has estimated her (and the other man). Geoffrey interests Brenda partly because he is sexually functional, but more because "he pays attention to me and he talks to me" (261).

Clearly, if a man loves a woman, he should pay attention to her and talk to her, but this novel at least *seems* to raise the question whether a man should love a woman in the first place. Certainly Jake, having been told that his condition is probably curable, thinks over all the women he has known and decides to pass up the treatment. In fact, "it was quite easy" (276).

Notes

1. Kingsley Amis, *Girl, 20* (New York: Harcourt Brace Jovanovich, 1972) 49. Further references are noted parenthetically in the text.

AMIS IN THE 1970s

2. He is comparable, in fact, to the faithless Russians in *Russian Hide-and-Seek* who fail to accomplish anything because they do not believe in anything.

3. Michael Barber, "The Art of Fiction LIX: Kingsley Amis," *Paris Review* 64 (1975): 70.

4. Kingsley Amis, *Ending Up* (New York: Harcourt Brace Jovanovich, 1974) 13; further references are noted parenthetically in the text. Adela, whose goodness is no match for her ugliness, is like Graham McClintoch in *Take a Girl Like You*.

5. Barber 69.

6. D. R. Wilmes, "When the Curse Begins to Hurt: Kingsley Amis and Satiric Confrontation," *Studies in Contemporary Satire* 5 (1978): 18.

7. Malcolm Bradbury, *No, Not Bloomsbury* (New York: Columbia University Press, 1988) 215; Philip Gardner, *Kingsley Amis* (Boston: Twayne, 1981) 105.

8. Kingsley Amis, *Jake's Thing* (New York: Viking Press, 1979) 216. Further references are noted parenthetically in the text.

9. Richard Bradford comments on this book by again decrying "the tendency for critics to interpret Amis's novels as straightforward outpourings of reaction, sexist, bigoted philistinism." *Kingsley Amis* (London: Edward Arnold, 1989) 15. See also John McDermott, "Kingsley and the Women," *Critical Quarterly* 27 (Autumn 1985) passim.

10. See Keith Wilson, "Jim, Jake and the Years Between: The Will to Stasis in the Contemporary British Novel," *Ariel* 13 (January 1982): 57, where Jake's outburst is related to Jim Dixon's abortive Merrie England lecture: like Jim, Jake "eventually, also aided by drink, manages to reconcile inner thoughts and outer statements in a swingeing denunciation of a cause he is supposed to be espousing."

CHAPTER SEVEN

Recent Novels

Since 1980 Amis's career has continued to demonstrate the kind of versatility and fertility which it has always shown. In the 1980s he published his collected short stories and an ambitious collection of his nonfiction, he edited a collection of science fiction, and he produced two books about drinking. In addition to *Russian Hide-and-Seek* and *The Crime of the Century*, discussed in Chapter 5, he has written and published since 1980 four mainstream novels: *Stanley and the Women*, *The Old Devils*, *Difficulties with Girls*, and *The Folks That Live on the Hill*. In 1991 he published his *Memoirs*.

The feeling of summing up and celebrating that is evident—if not in the novels, then in the *Memoirs* and the collections of nonfiction and short fiction—also appears in his society's response to him. In 1981 he was made a Commander of the British Empire, and in 1990 he was knighted, both by the government of Margaret Thatcher, whom Amis admires and even finds quite sexy.[1] In 1986 his novel *The Old Devils* was chosen for the Booker Prize, the most prestigious award for fiction in Britain. In recent years, perhaps stimulated by the Booker Prize and his honors, many of his books have been

RECENT NOVELS

reprinted in paperback editions (some, like *Lucky Jim,* have never been out of print), and in other ways the publishing world has suggested that he is newly important: for instance, in the publication of *A Kingsley Amis Omnibus* (1987), which combines *Jake's Thing, The Old Devils,* and *Stanley and the Women.*

Stanley and the Women (1984)

Perhaps because of higher visibility, too, but certainly also because of the perceived misogyny of some of his characters, and arguably of himself, Amis also became more controversial in the 1980s.[2] Already in *Jake's Thing* reviewers were beginning to point to a troubling sense that something was wrong with women as a group, according to Amis. His work has always contained its share of "awful" women (beginning with Margaret in *Lucky Jim*), but then the world contains awful women; Amis's books also have featured many *more* awful men, and the norm of goodness, common sense, unselfishness, and clear thinking has, more often than not, been a woman like Christine in *Lucky Jim* or Helene Bang in *One Fat Englishman.*

Beginning with *Jake's Thing* and accelerating very much with *Stanley and the Women,* the question of Amis and the women has been raised more insistently, as, in these books, the relevant male characters are far more likely to denounce women, usually for unreliability of emotion, refusal to speak plainly, and a desire to "fuck up" men. Moreover, the range of female characters seems to have narrowed a bit, so that, in fact, the normative women, the ones who see through the heroes and set them right and set an example of right feeling and normal fidelity and Christian kindness—these women are in shorter supply. Now of course, readers differ widely on whether the attitudes expressed by Amis's characters, even his central characters, are shared by the author—a challenge posed as far back as Jim Dixon's distaste for Mozart, dismissal of Graham Greene, and other "anti-intellectualisms." When Amis tells an interviewer that "Jake's problems are not mine," he may seem to be distancing himself from Jake's growing conviction that women are not enough to justify having a sex drive.[3] Or he may simply be asserting that *his* thing still works.

In two different treatments of the problem, both called "Kingsley and the Women," John McDermott and Hermione Lee address Amis's attitudes and come to widely differing conclusions. McDermott is writing about *Jake's Thing* and Lee is reviewing *Difficulties with Girls*, but in their titles both reveal the centrality of *Stanley and the Women* to this inquiry. McDermott provides a long list of good and attractive women in Amis's work, along with the much shorter list of awful ones, and concludes that Amis is not to be held responsible for Jake's misogyny; rather, that he falls into the familiar Amis category, the "hero-as-shit."[4] Not only that, but impatience with women is, with Jake, part of a growing impatience with almost everything, brought on by aging and fear of death. Thus, he concludes, "Jake's thing is . . . *Jake's* thing, not Amis's, and, although antipathy to women is a marked symp-

tom of the condition, the thing itself, as is shown by the music
of elegy in the passage last quoted [a memory of a time when
Jake felt emotions about something that now leaves him cold],
is more than is simply suggested by 'misogyny': Jake's thing is
that nothing now seems worth the effort."[5]

Hermione Lee sees it all very differently. Not only is the
chief characteristic of Amis's more recent novels a genuine hatred of women, but she is also certain, without saying why,
that it is Amis's own feeling: "However reprehensible the
main character, he is always the Amis-surrogate whose assumptions are lined up like his author's. . . . "[6] As for *Stanley
and the Women*, it is described by one reviewer, Val Hennessy,
as having been "written by someone who harbours a patho-
logical hatred of women."[7]

The story of *Stanley and the Women* is simple. Stanley
Duke, the advertising manager of a daily newspaper in London, lives in a fashionable part of town with his fashionable
wife, Susan, who is the assistant literary editor of another
newspaper. Susan comes from the upper class—her mother is
Lady Daly—while Stanley has risen from working-class, presumably somewhat Cockney origins, somewhere south of the
Thames. His real interests are cars and drinking in pubs, and
he and his wife seem to get along well enough. Both have been
married before.

The story begins with the irruption into their lives of
Stanley's grown son, Steve, who, instead of being abroad as
they thought, has stayed in London and gone mad. There is no
question here that Steve really is mad; he suffers from delusions, babbles about conspiracies of the Jews, climbs up in a

UNDERSTANDING KINGSLEY AMIS

tree and won't come down, and so on. When he first appears, he is running water pointlessly all over the kitchen floor. Stanley's first, normal, response is to get him help, and, summoning a doctor friend, he gets Steve into psychiatric care.

Here the trouble begins. Steve's mother, Stanley's ex-wife Nowell, an actress who has remarried and now has a little girl, must be brought into the case, and she and Stanley cannot get along; nor can Nowell's new husband, one Bert Hutchinson, seem to tolerate Stanley. There are several examples of Nowell's selfishness and unwillingness to take any responsibility for Steve. Then Steve's psychiatrist turns out to be a woman. Dr. Trish Collings pursues a course of treatment that seems to combine wrong diagnosis, desire to blame Stanley for Steve's problems, and fashionably liberated thinking in about equal measure; she sees Steve's madness as part of a process by which "kids learn to express themselves and develop their identities."[8] She encourages him to return to Stanley's house before he shows any apparent sign of improvement (rather the reverse, as he starts to seem almost catatonic as well as deluded). Her hostility to Stanley, which is manifested as a tendency to blame him for Steve's condition, becomes more and more naked, and she finally threatens to throw an untreated Steve back on his hands if Stanley doesn't shape up.

Steve's condition imperils relations between Stanley and Susan, aided by her mother's and sister's intervention; finally, a disputed event brings matters to a climax. Susan reports that the recently re-released Steve has attacked her with a knife, wounding her arm. Steve goes back to the mental hospital, but Stanley's wondering whether the wound might not have been

RECENT NOVELS

inflicted by Susan herself to get rid of Steve leads to an as-
tonishing outburst; beginning by calling him "bastard. Swine.
Filth," she escalates to this: " 'Yer, ass right, the wife's gorn
orf to er muvver's' she said in a very poor imitation of perhaps
a Hackney or Bow accent as much as anything. 'Just up your
street, you lower-class turd. I don't know how I've put up with
you for so long, with your gross table-manners and your booz-
ing and your bloody little car and your frightful *mates* and your
whole ghastly south-of-the-river man's world. You've no
breeding and so you've no respect for women' " (217).
Though she does in fact leave, before much longer Steve is
back in the hospital, and Susan has phoned and wants to come
back to Stanley. This is where it ends.

The main interest in the book, as the title indicates, is in
Stanley's relations with women. Clearly, he has married two
troublesome ones, unable to see beyond their own interests;
Bert Hutchinson, with whom Stanley has a long talk about
Nowell, suggests that her only motive is using men. Stanley
also has particularly bad luck when Trish Collings becomes
Steve's psychiatrist. These are all explicable in the statistical
probability of finding damaging women in London.

Sometimes women themselves deliver the diagnosis of
feminine malevolence, though they are only talking about
some women. Stanley and Susan's friend Lindsey Lucas tells
him that Susan is mad, impossibly competitive, and mostly interested in attention-grabbing. Likewise, Mrs. Shillabeer, the
housekeeper, adds her own theory: "Stanley, you're a darling,
you are. No, it's that stuck-up cat you married. What did you
want to go and do that for, a nice guy like you? . . . You want

to watch the mother. That's the way Susan'll end up. Well, she's most of the way there already, I reckon'' (207).

What elevates Stanley's case beyond a series of unhappy relationships with women is the many conversations in the book that argue for a malignant conspiracy among women to harm men. Dr. Nash, the first psychiatrist to examine Steve, and the one who finally rescues him from Dr. Collings, asks Stanley in their first conversation: ''Would you say, would you assent to the proposition that all women are mad?'' (57), and Stanley reasonably says, no, not all of them. During the course of the book, he seems driven to change his mind, as he discovers the winding mental ways of his current and former wives. After the stabbing and Susan's departure; after comments like Stanley's, ''He covered up his disappointment like a man, meaning none of it showed'' (230); after a chat with his editor, who tells him how much simpler it is to hire prostitutes than to marry so that there is no necessity to talk to women or spend the money marriage costs—after all this, there is a final long conversation with Dr. Nash, who delivers what at least *seems* to be accredited as authorial wisdom. Now he says that the trouble is that women are not mad, so they cannot be cured, and he overflows with this:

> ''Not enough of a motive?'' His voice had gone very high. ''Fucking up a man? Not enough of a motive? What are you talking about? Good God, you've had wives, haven't you? . . . You must have suffered before from the effect of their having noticed, at least the brighter ones among them having noticed, that men are different, men quite often

wonder whether they're doing the right thing and worry
about it, men have been known to blame themselves for behaving badly, men not only feel they've made mistakes but
on occasion will actually admit having done so, and say
they're sorry, and ask to be forgiven, and promise not to do
it again, and mean it. Think of that! Mean it. All beyond
female comprehension. Which incidentally is why they're
not novelists and must never be priests. Not enough of a
motive? They don't have motives as you and I understand
them. They have the means and the opportunity, that is
enough." (246–47)

Stanley goes immediately to his childhood friend, Cliff Wain-
wright, who gives him a further installment, including his
wonderment that only twenty-five percent of English husbands batter their wives. Stanley arrives at this *aperçu:* "In
fact women only want one thing, for men to want to fuck
them" (254).

Figuring out what to think about these views provides the
problem for readers. A look at the structure of the novel,
though, seems to suggest that these views are, in some way,
the novel's thesis. Stanley arrives at them after what looks like
a struggle, and finally there is no one to argue against them.
The men (perhaps the "ghastly south-of-the-river man's
world" Susan dislikes?) are in agreement on this one, and the
women are offstage. As D. A. N. Jones says, "There is no
stern judge to rebuke Stanley."[9] Even Susan's apologetic
phone call to Stanley, with which the book closes, seems like
another attempt, having damaged him by leaving, to damage
him again by coming back.

Besides being structured as if to press a thesis, this novel is uncharacteristically humorless for an Amis book. Challenged by Val Hennessy on this point, the author says, "It has its funny parts. The mad youth's absurd delusions are funny. Can't you see that tragedy and humour can be very close? . . . Certainly funny."[10] Though tragedy and comedy certainly *can* be very close, they are not automatically so. This book, which at least seems to set up an absurd theory—women's conspiracy against men—as a reasonable corrective to Steve's *mad* theory of the Jewish conspiracy against Gentiles, contains the satiric aim of more successful Amis books like *Girl, 20*. But it has a leaden tone that dulls the satire and militates against what Amis is presumably aiming at, as in all his novels: a book that entertains readers while taking a serious moral stance.

The Old Devils (1986)

His next novel, which won Amis his first Booker Prize, is his best work since *Ending Up*. Like that book, it observes the changes which result from growing older with a mixture of acidity and comedy. It, too, is an ensemble book, with a large cast of characters and no clear protagonist. It embodies the strengths of all Amis's best books: clearly observed persons and traits, wittily rendered; humor; a sharp eye for pretension and cant; strong and clear emotion. At the heart of it, as is usually the case, is the sexual relationship—that is, the relations between men and women, including sexual intercourse but including much else as well.

RECENT NOVELS

For a study of pretension and artificiality, Amis appears to believe, what better locale than Wales? He seems to see Wales as a place that encourages people to posture and Welshness as a trait almost impossible to possess naturally. Like John Lewis, who is a Welshman impatient with the excesses of his compatriots in *That Uncertain Feeling,* the characters in this novel are all Welsh, and yet most of them derive no great warmth from that fact. Exceptions are Malcolm Cellan-Davies, who is sentimental, translates Welsh verse, and takes a dignified Welsh-patriotic, if not Welsh-nationalist, stand; and Alun Weaver, a sort of professional Welshman whose career has been partly parasitic on *another* professional Welshman, the poet Brydan. In Brydan, Amis creates another quasi-Dylan Thomas figure, subject to the same sort of scrutiny as Amis has expressed in his nonfiction accounts of his dealings with Thomas and in the figure of Gareth Probert in *I Like It Here.*

But most of the bluster and posturing are transferred to Alun Weaver, author of *Brydan's Wales,* a writer and broadcaster in London for many years who, as this novel opens, has decided to come back to make his home in Wales. The suspicions of Alun are voiced by one character who says, ''When anyone wants a colourful kind of stage-Taffy view on this and that then of course they go to him. With a bit of eloquent sobstuff thrown in at Christmas or when it's dogs or the poor. He's the up-market media Welshman.''[11] On arrival, Alun unleashes (into a television camera) a paean to Wales that includes such pseudo-Dylanisms as the following: Wales means ''Many things grave and gay and multi-coloured but one above all: I'm coming home. . . . Heart is where the home is, and the heart of a Welshman . . . '' (42).

But Alun Weaver is more than a Welsh imposter. He is like most of the large cast in this book, a mixed character, who has some good impulses hidden among normal human traits like selfishness and dishonesty and a few that are particular to himself: a vanity that probably rests on a bedrock of self-doubt about his abilities, and a relentless philandering that may well have the same origin.

The return to Wales of Alun Weaver and his wife, Rhiannon, is the stimulus for most of what happens in *The Old Devils*. But it is less the effect on them (though that is considerable, arguably including Alun's death) that is most interesting in this book, but the way it brings out traits, comic and otherwise, in the residents of the town. There is a group of locals, almost all of them lifelong residents, who are friendly with each other and related in other ways as well. All are getting old—that is, in their early or middle sixties. The men, none of whom has a real job to go to, habitually gather at the Bible and Crown pub, where they have a sort of club, to pass their days in talk and drinking. The talk is often enough about the effects of time and age—about people their age or younger who have died or about the degeneracy of modern times, including young people, women in pubs, and rock music. Meanwhile, the women meet in someone's home for a "coffee morning" and also talk and drink. Amis's books have always contained plenty of drinking, but nothing comparable to this one, especially in terms of women's drunkenness. From time to time, the two groups overlap—for instance, at public ceremonies or weddings or when a man picks his wife up at her coffee morning—but for the most part there is a men's world and a separate women's world. Most of the married couples are settled but hardly *happy*; this seems a standard feature of life here, rather than a consequence of women's or men's malice. The separation of men and women gives Alun Weaver the opportunity he needs both to evade his wife and to visit the wives of his friends for sexual liaisons.

The complicated nexus of relationships is best illustrated by Peter Thomas, a grossly fat member of the men's drinking club, who, along with Charlie Norris, seems to see most clearly and certainly comments most acidly on the people and events around them. Peter, apparently a retired lecturer, is married to Muriel, the only non-native; long in the past, he had had an affair with Rhiannon Weaver, making her pregnant, but leaving her (after an abortion) for another woman, who, it is later disclosed, was Angharad, now wife of Garth Pumphrey, an eccentric and less-well-liked habitué of the Bible and Crown. Alun Weaver, in addition to being married to Rhiannon, has affairs with the wives of Charlie and Malcolm. Malcolm is and always has been hopelessly in love with Rhiannon. Peter's son marries the daughter of Alun and Rhiannon Weaver.

The novel moves along, providing glimpses of all these people interacting with each other, fuelled by the usual high level of drinking and sarcastic observations by the more intelligent and/or detached among them. The most momentous events are little enough. Alun organizes a trip out to the countryside, in the course of which Malcolm is beaten by thuggish bartenders after trying to stand up for Wales. Alun sleeps with one woman and another, believing entirely without justice that he is fooling everybody. Malcolm takes Rhiannon for a drive

to the seashore and touchingly tells her his love. Alun organizes another outing, this time with Charlie and his wife, to
Brydan's home town; there he asks Charlie to give him an
honest evaluation of his writing about Wales, receives it, and
vengefully subjects Charlie to a shattering fright. (This is the
sort of telling detail that shows the reader that Alun is not just
a high-spirited, full-of-himself literary man, but a self-
absorbed person with few decent human impulses, or, as Peter's son calls him after he is dead, a "frightful shit" [282].)

The most important sequence of events is tragicomic, like
the book itself. Alun Weaver joins the men's drinking club at
the Bible and Crown but cannot resist denouncing the landlord
as "the kind of idiot who's ruining Wales" (250), getting
them all banned from the pub. They go along to Garth Pumphrey's mausoleum-like house, where none of them have ever
been, have a spooky few moments leading up to the revelation
that they have to buy drinks from him, and watch as Alun,
poising himself for a wounding sally against Garth, drops dead
instead.

The coda of the novel is the wedding of William Thomas
and Rosemary Weaver. This is as close as the novel comes to
a happy outcome—both the young people are nice, wise, unaffected—and it provides the occasion for summings-up all
around. Muriel announces she is leaving Peter, Garth says
complimentary things about Alun Weaver which he may believe but no one else can, and there is even a bit of nude horse-
play among the elderly guests. People drink a great deal. Most
importantly, Peter and Rhiannon have a clearing-the-air talk,
in which he apologizes for letting her down years ago and, it

is clear, their relations are put on something like the old footing (so much that he moves in with her). The happy wedding, with good prospects for Peter and Rhiannon as well, is a sunny conclusion to the book, though it is an autumnal sunshine. (Jill Farringdon compares this book to "a contemporary *Winter's Tale*."[12]) Here, too, someone sums up the problem of Welshness which has occupied a good deal of conversation through this novel: "Wales is a subject that can't be talked about. Unless you're making a collection of dishonesty and self-deception and sentimental bullshit" (284).

Though the wedding has nothing to do with Alun's death, the way it immediately follows it in the book suggests a thematic connection. Obviously, it clears the way for Peter and Rhiannon. But it also seems to have functioned for these Welsh characters as catalyst for other changes, some of them only temporary, it is true. It leads to one of the most unambiguous happy endings Amis has written in many years. It even suggests a revaluation of the dynamics of the novel. There are many characters with parts of roughly equal size, and the omniscient narration of the book gives the reader inside views of the thoughts of most or all of them, so no one person seems to figure as central; Alun Weaver, because of his *activity*, comes to look like the main character (hardly the hero). But by the end of the book, a more careful look shows that Rhiannon, on whom Amis seldom focuses and who says and does little, is really the moral heart of this novel. Her behavior at the wedding and even the short chapter after it that shows Malcolm writing a poem to her, make her luminous, above the petty lives of the rest of the old devils. And, though

Alun Weaver sometimes thinks, self-defensively, of how women try to ruin things for men—a line of argument familiar from *Stanley and the Women*—in this novel such a thought becomes another detail of his own moral meanness, and Rhiannon takes her place alongside Jenny Bunn and Catherine Casement as a sexually desirable woman who is also as close as the novel lets anyone come to goodness and wisdom.

Difficulties with Girls (1988)

Jenny Bunn, now married to Patrick Standish, makes her reappearance in Amis's next novel, *Difficulties with Girls*. In a 1974 interview, when asked what the lives of Jenny and Patrick would be like after *Take a Girl Like You*, he answered, "He'll marry her and bugger off"[13] The exposition of the past that brings events up to date in this book, which is set in 1967, shows that that is not exactly what happened, though it is close enough, and its point, that Patrick is unreliable and selfish, is amply borne out by the sequel. Jenny had become pregnant, presumably when Patrick's rape in *Take a Girl Like You* led to a more regular sexual relationship. They married. She miscarried. Since that time, she has been unable to conceive, though she wants children. Patrick has left school-teaching and has taken a job with a publisher, a job he earned by drunken charm at a party. They now live in London. Jenny no longer teaches school but works teaching children in a hospital.

The time is of course the swinging 1960s, and Amis has laid on many period details. There is an Indian guru in Eaton

Terrace. Patrick's publisher looks for trendy books like *The Mode is the Meaning,* by "Mabuse," to show that he is an "uncontrollably go-ahead publisher," and talks about "feedback" and a book as "a commodity like any other."[14] The sexual revolution figures here as well; women are much more "emancipated" than in the period when Patrick and Jenny first met, and homosexuality is more open as well; though animosity to homosexuals is also rife, the passage of the Act of Parliament decriminalizing homosexual acts between adult men occurs in the course of the novel. A homosexual couple lives in the flat next to Patrick and Jenny.

In fact, the whole atmosphere is highly sexualized, and the novel is, as the title announces, about various kinds of difficulties with girls. One sort, loosely speaking, might be that experienced by the homosexuals Eric and Stevie, who of course are not interested in girls sexually; moreover, Patrick, trying to explain homosexual life to another man, identifies Stevie, whose acting career is based on his rugged virility in films, as the female member of the couple: "The one who went on about being hard done by and got annoyed and attracted all the attention and broke up the party and generally behaved badly is the pretty one. You've had quite enough to do with women to be able to take that in" (106). The person he is speaking to, Tim Vatcher, also has difficulties with girls; a married man, he has left his wife and is moving into the block of flats where the Standishes live (called Lower Ground) to start anew, and he is thinking of starting over as a homosexual.

But the main difficulties with girls afflict Patrick and Jenny. Patrick is self-indulgent to a fault, cannot restrain himself from ogling and commenting on other women and in fact fairly often going to bed with them. He is troubled by two women in this novel, the predatory Barbara Giles, wife of Patrick's boss, and Wendy Porter-King, a neighbor in Lower Ground, with whom he does have an affair, having told Jenny just before its inception that he isn't interested. Patrick is an odd sort who expects commendation if he is faithful to Jenny, and to that end he tells her that he has considered sleeping with Wendy but decided against it—to elicit her gratitude. When he has been unfaithful, he stops short of thinking he has done nothing wrong, but is tenderly forgiving of himself. In general, though several years have passed, Patrick has not matured beyond where he left off in *Take a Girl Like You*.

Jenny has the most worrying difficulties with girls— other girls who come to Patrick's attention. She reacts fatalistically when she sees Barbara Giles at a party; "Breasts had brought Jenny a peck of trouble over the years" (16), and she recognizes the signs of Patrick's interest in Barbara and, later, his having reached a quick understanding with Wendy Porter-King. She can hardly leave him alone at a party for ten minutes. It is after her discovery of the Wendy affair—which has crossed some invisible line, proving that there is no taboo Patrick recognizes, even one suggesting he keep his philandering away from their home—that Jenny leaves him for a few days. But after some inconclusive events that hardly prove him repentant or improved, she comes back.

It is then that Patrick escalates his operations and proves that he understands Jenny's scruples more poorly, even after seven years of marriage, than any moderately alert reader of

RECENT NOVELS

Take a Girl Like You. Taking Jenny to a party, he introduces her to an attractive man with whom, it becomes clear, he is trying to maneuver her into sleeping. No Amis protagonist who really cares about a woman wants to share her; surely, this is the point made so clearly about Douglas Yandell in *Girl, 20*. Patrick's scheme presumably may be part of the swinging 1960s atmosphere of "letting it all hang out"; and Simon Giles has been trying to find a lover for his wife, who has been reading "Anthea Schmutzige's *Trigger My Bomb*" and is now more than he can satisfy (261). More likely, of course, this is Patrick's way of salving his own conscience, of putting Jenny equally in the wrong with him. Naturally, she rejects it.

Amis's decision to revisit Jenny and Patrick is an interesting one. *Take a Girl Like You* was his first novel to incorporate an essentially non-comic examination of sexual relationships and a step forward in reaching a somewhat inconclusive, bittersweet ending. Both these features have become more and more characteristic of the Amis novel in the succeeding three decades. Moreover, the earlier book was a sociologically interesting look at a specific society in a specific time and its shifting mores—the period of affluence and youth and growing hedonism that followed the war and the long postwar privation. In *Difficulties with Girls*, he is again examining a period through the microcosm of a couple.

In the sequel, there are reminders, some of them fairly detachable, of the original book. Graham McClintoch comes to London to visit and tut-tuts about declining standards and moral laxity. He has taken a new position, as "Head of Chemistry Studies"—a title that (by being "softer" than "Head of

Chemistry'') reveals to him the Decline of the West. More-over, he has married and, as would have been predicted from his speech to Jenny about ugly people marrying ugly people because of the gulf that separates them from the handsome, his wife is indescribable. Patrick looks at her photograph and thinks that she "was not especially old or ugly or evil-looking, just very hard to take in as married to anyone you knew, though as a rabies victim's estranged wife, say, glimpsed while turning through the newspaper—no problem'' (191).

But the invitation to compare *Difficulties with Girls* with *Take a Girl Like You* ultimately shows how much better the earlier book is. It is both funnier and sadder, more imaginative and more realistic. By 1988, both Jenny and Patrick have lost complexity, become less fully dimensional. In aging, Patrick has become more unpleasant; he has moved to the right polit-ically, as Amis did at his age, and he now expresses late-Amis-style attitudes about women. For instance, he reflects that "it was one of Graham's great virtues that when he said he was sorry he sounded sorry, not huffy. But then he was a bloke'' (195). Patrick is the self-confidently knowing—perhaps ''cocksure'' is the right term here—man who is just too much of a sport to be faithful to his wife. Jenny is, much too much, the good woman loving and waiting for her tearaway husband, and little more. That she leaves him suggests possibly inter-esting new directions; that she returns puts an end to them.

The mechanisms by which all this happens are at the same time reminiscent of *Take a Girl Like You* and stagy, al-most careless. In the earlier novel, Jenny's love for Patrick will not permit her to cut him loose even though he is unfaithful; he

RECENT NOVELS

finally rapes her while she is drunk. Then, in a climactic fury, she shows that she knows how unworthy he is—that he is a coward, a sneak, a snob, as well as a sexual cad—and she makes it up with him anyway. In *Difficulties with Girls,* she leaves him and, after a few days, comes back; there follows a flurry of activity, including Tim's trying out the homosexual life, to his disgust, and a knife fight between Eric and Stevie, which Tim breaks up while Patrick, cowardly as ever, hides; the Standishes' cat comes home; Patrick devises the plan for Jenny to have an affair, and she denounces him, again, during the course of which she tells him:

> "I don't think I can go on loving you indefinitely, not like this. Of course, we might get on better that way. Then you could be a shit to your heart's content."
> "Is there any hope for us?"
> "Not as we are. Not unless something happens. And I don't see anything happening." (239)

And then it does happen. Jenny learns that she is pregnant, and Patrick responds "You've done it. Changed everything. You've saved us" (276). This seems an odd sort of a solution to problems that seem to be entirely of Patrick's making, and its very triteness, its predictability in a certain kind of book (not the kind of book, either, that one expects from Kingsley Amis) arouse the suspicion of irony. Jenny is smart enough to reflect that this will save them but only for a few years, but even that qualification does not answer the questions this ending raises. Patrick never longs for children, and to propose that his defective love for Jenny (who, it is always stipulated, is beautiful and so sexually desirable that men cannot leave her alone and women suspect her on sight) has been healed and elevated by her pregnancy seems formulaic to say the least. Patrick explains at one point "shitty things are always simple. Same as great things. Patrick Standish, in conversation" (248). In *Difficulties with Girls* Jenny and Patrick, and the moral choices their actions create, and perhaps even life itself, have been simplified too much.

The Folks That Live on the Hill (1990)

Amis's most recent novel—set, as references in the text make clear, in 1990—has a much more genial tone than *Difficulties with Girls*. There is the occasional anti-female blast; for instance, among a list of things that have gotten worse, particularly in pubs, comes this explanation: the people who ruin pubs "all tended to fall into the same categories, like no-hopers, louts and often sheer kids, meaning young kids, also females who brought the kids into the place with them as one way of demolishing another bit of blokes' territory, a more wholesale way than just coming in themselves."[15] This thought is attributed to Desmond, a crude—though likeable, on the whole—restaurateur whose wife has left him to take up a lesbian life, to his invincible wonder. Nevertheless, the tone of this book is less acid than some recent ones, and the diminished wariness about the motivations and limitations of *all women* is an important part of it.

Even the title has a more relaxed feeling to it, and it gestures toward the kind of book this is. Though it has a main

RECENT NOVELS

character, Harry Caldecote, it is also an ensemble portrait of
people who are loosely held together by living near each other,
in the ''Shepherd's Hill'' section of London. This is an urban
neighborhood, in which people know each other and much of
the action requires them to meet each other in the post office
(with two Indian brothers, carefully characterized by Amis
and used as something like a chorus), the local liquor store,
and, most importantly, the pub, called the King's. Not all the
characters live in Shepherd's Hill, though. What they really
have in common is a greater or lesser degree of dependence on
Harry Caldecote.

Harry is one of the most interesting protagonists Amis
has created in some time. He is kind and optimistic, though
never simple-minded or soft-headed (in fact, he has a simple-
minded, soft-headed brother Freddie around, by comparison
with whom he seems positively Machiavellian). He is amply
supplied with the arsenal of Amisian prejudices and dislikes,
particularly of trendy or youthfully fashionable things, either
modes of speech, ways of dress, or kinds of behavior (e.g.,
openly lesbian ménages). Instead of denouncing other people,
in the Roger Micheldene or Alun Weaver manner, he keeps
most of his critical thoughts to himself, as most Amis protagonists do, but these thoughts are fairly unsparing; after his un-
loved sister-in-law, Désirée, says of her husband (Harry's
brother Freddie): ''I just happen to love him,'' Harry reflects:

Although she laid no special stress on the last word, Désirée pronounced it with a full initial aspirate. To Harry
Caldecote, this on its own stamped her not only as an ir-
remediable third-rate genteelist bullshitter, along with those

who talked of tissyou paper and yesterdae and one's fawhed, but in the present context as one who could only be pretending to feel the emotion she alleged. But he came no closer to confiding this to her than to bawling at her that nobody *just happened* to love anybody. (30–31)

Despite his being amply accredited by his author with a long nose for hypocrisy and deceit, the surprising fact is that Harry Caldecote is a philanthrope, almost a professional one. This book is full of no-hopers and dysfunctional people, all of whom look to Harry, and, despite his not wanting to, he takes responsibility for them. Speaking of Freddie, he complains, ''I don't know, I keep feeling responsible for people and there doesn't seem to be anything I can do about it'' (12).

The novel is loosely constructed as a series of encounters which gradually reveal the circumstances of all the people for whom Harry feels responsible. In this respect, *The Folks That Live on the Hill* paints quite a bleak landscape of contemporary urban life. Harry feels responsible for Bunty Streatfield; he has stood up for her (''taken her on,'' in a phrase that Amis uses elsewhere—for instance in *Girl, 20*—to mean ''accepted responsibility for her even at the cost of trouble to himself''), first when she married a man her family disliked, then when she left him and took up with a domineering lesbian named Popsy. Almost impartially, he also feels responsible for the estranged husband, Desmond, and helps him and Bunty towards some sort of reconciliation, a more-than-friendship that acknowledges Bunty's sexual feelings, before the conclusion of the book. Harry stops short of accepting Popsy, though he is

RECENT NOVELS

otherwise catholic in his efforts; Popsy is repulsive in many ways—for instance, Harry encounters her once as "a kind of elderly small boy dressed like a conscript in some half-starved oriental army" (71), and she strikes another observer as suggesting "some small gnawing mammal like a beaver" (119)—but what puts her beyond the pale is her malice. She wilfully hurts Bunty, finally even beating her up. This is a book about kindness, or tolerance, in a difficult world.

Harry also has a niece by marriage, Fiona Carr-Stewart, whose life is much more wretched; a terrible alcoholic who spends much of every day drunk and who is in and out of hospitals (at Harry's expense), she has seduced all the cab drivers in her district, as well as gas meter-readers and other casual passersby; Harry is unsurprised to receive phone calls from remote and frightening-sounding bars all over greater London informing him that Fiona is on the kitchen floor and requesting that he do something about it. Fiona is a carefully drawn character, someone for whom the dark side of Amis's habitual celebration of drinking (and even of drunkenness, in inimitable comic passages) is the only side there is. She loathes herself, considers suicide, goes on the wagon only to fall off it. Harry learns that Fiona feels fated to destroy her life because she has purportedly discovered that she is identical to her aunt Annie, who ruined her life in a similar way; he is able to show her that the similarity does not exist, that the determinism Fiona feels is not there.

Closer to home, Harry has a mother, to whom he shows the normal attentions; a widowed sister, Clare, whom he has taken in as a companion/housekeeper; a brother, Freddie, who has a wife, Désirée, and a son, Piers. Freddie's problem is that he cannot control his own life because Désirée is too powerful for him. Harry is able to encourage Freddie to write poetry, specifying that he must have privacy to write and must not discuss his magnum opus with *anyone* until it is complete. Having given Freddie some freedom from Désirée, he later even finds a publisher for the poem (to his surprise, since it is no good), permitting Freddie to earn a considerable sum of money for himself.

Piers, the adult son, is a wastrel and a sponger. Freddie houses him, in the same flat he has provided for Bunty and Popsy, and both Freddie and Clare give Piers handouts. Piers is apparently in his middle thirties; but, though he does not deserve to be supported, particularly given his own pretensions of gentility, Harry helps him whenever he can. It is when Piers asks for 50,000 pounds for an investment— apparently, in stolen vodka—and Harry refuses that Piers involves others, including Harry's mother and his brother Freddie, who invests his entire royalty payments. This, like almost everything else in the novel, works out. Against the odds, Piers really does make a substantial profit on the investment; Freddie now has money that Désirée knows nothing about, with which to pursue his secret vice of stamp-collecting; and Piers is rich, presumably independent, and newly engaged to an upper-class girl who is an old friend of the newly dried-out Fiona.

The blemish on Harry's routine is provided by an invitation for him to move to America and be a visiting professor at a place in the Northwest called the Adams Institute. (The

novel makes clear that Harry, in addition to having some
money and being somewhat posh, is quite a famous man, con-
sidering that he is a retired librarian.) He finds various reasons
to argue with himself against taking the post, including that
the state is full of hicks, and so on, but is almost persuaded to
go until Clare asks him to stay. It is clear that to go to America
would be to sever himself from the various waifs and misfits
for whom he feels responsible, and so it is not surprising that
he cannot.

Harry Caldecote is a fine creation, a magisterial figure
like Prospero in *The Tempest*. The novel revolves around him
and his manipulation, in the best sense, of a variety of needy
people (at one point Harry says quite penetratingly, "Holding
people in play is my natural game" [81]), and the needy people and their needs are funny or sad, or both. The people
Harry holds in play all improve their conditions by the end of
the book. He complains about being unable to stop feeling responsibility for people for whom he really has no responsibility, but his decision to stay in England clearly demonstrates
that when given a chance to sever his various webs of sympathy and assistance he would really rather not. Harry's credo
makes for an interesting summary of the book, especially con-
sidering the particular resonance "awful" has always had for
Amis as a judgment on people like Roger Micheldene: "I
don't think there are any really *bad* people. Just awful ones.
The bad ones are all in books" (89). Harry is a man surrounded by people of varying degrees of awfulness, and his
forbearance and willingness to "take them on" marks him as
a genuinely good man.

UNDERSTANDING KINGSLEY AMIS

Notes

1. Kingsley Amis, *Memoirs* (New York: Summit Books, 1991) 316.

2. John McDermott comments perceptively on these reasons. *Kingsley Amis: An English Moralist* (New York: St. Martin's, 1989) 218–19.

3. John McDermott, "Kingsley and the Women," *Critical Quarterly* 27 (Autumn 1985): 65.

4. McDermott, "Kingsley and the Women" 67.

5. McDermott, "Kingsley and the Women" 71.

6. Hermione Lee, "Kingsley and the Women," *The New Republic* 201 (July 31, 1989): 40.

7. Val Hennessy, *A Little Light Friction* (London: Futura Publications, 1989) 203.

8. Kingsley Amis, *Stanley and the Women* (New York: Summit Books, 1985) 126. Further references are noted parenthetically in the text.

9. D. A. N. Jones, "Kingsley Amis," *Grand Street* 4 (Spring 1985): 211.

10. Hennessy 206–7.

11. Kingsley Amis, *The Old Devils* (New York: Summit Books, 1987) 14. Further references are noted parenthetically in the text.

12. Jill Farringdon, "When You Come Home Again to Wales: Kingsley Amis's *The Old Devils*," *The Anglo-Welsh Review* 86 (1987): 91.

13. Clive James, "Profile 4: Kingsley Amis," *The New Review* 1 (July 1974): 24.

14. Kingsley Amis, *Difficulties with Girls* (New York: Summit Books, 1988) 46, 50. Further references are noted parenthetically in the text.

15. Kingsley Amis, *The Folks That Live on the Hill* (New York: Summit Books, 1991) 98–99. Further references are noted parenthetically in the text.

CONCLUSION

Garnet Bowen, the writer working as a "sham-detector" in *I Like It Here,* reads a couple of pages of a manuscript by a Henry James-like, high-modernist expatriate aesthete and decides he "wanted to put the man who had written that in the stocks and stand in front of him with a peck, or better a bushel, of ripe tomatoes and throw one at him for each time he failed to justify any phrase in the . . . scene on grounds of clarity, common sense, emotional decency and general morality."[1] This is a telling passage. One thing it points to is the generally corrective function of Amis's fiction. One thing that a novel does is say to the reader, "Life's not like that; it's like *this.*" Garnet Bowen voices Amis's objection to a view of life that his own fiction seems written in part to correct, as well as a *style* of writing that, particularly in its indifference to clarity, Amis indignantly rejects.

More important is the list of qualities he wants to see embodied in fiction: common sense, emotional decency and general morality. Though included in a denunciation rather than a manifesto, these are the qualities of Amis's own work at its best. His most recent novel, *The Folks That Live on the Hill,* demonstrates the author's determination to write about—to demonstrate—and to *value* clarity, common sense and emotional decency.

Common sense is closely connected with the comic, which, though not enumerated by Garnet Bowen, is a key component of almost everything Amis has written. Comedy, or humor, arises from the perception of distance between the real and the ideal, or between the real and the pretended, and the funny dramatization of that distance. The possessor of common sense is, like Garnet Bowen, a sham-detector. Detecting shams and provoking the reader to laugh at them is at the heart of Kingsley Amis's work.

Though he spoke in 1975 of the desirability of making his "bad people" ridiculous[2]—that is, of using his comedy in the interest of his "general morality"—it is helpful to correct this notion with Harry Caldecote's remark: "I don't think there are any really *bad* people. Just awful ones. The bad ones are all in books."[3]

In one sense, Harry is too generous, for Amis has included people in his books who *are bad*—for instance, Dr. Best in *The Anti-Death League* or possibly Sy via in *Girl, 20*. But in general the distinction he makes between bad people and awful ones is appropriate and useful in understanding Kingsley Amis. Awful people (those for whom Amis has tended to use the label "bastards") are selfish or obtuse, racist or sexist, drunken or lecherous, above all hypocritical or vain or pretentious; but they are not *evil*. If they were evil, they would be beyond the author's (or reader's) powers of sympathy, and few of Amis's characters really are completely beyond sympathy. Even worse, they would be inappropriate objects of humor. Fielding (identified by Garnet Bowen as an inspirational figure) explained that hypocrisy and affectation are appropriate objects of ridicule, while true evil (much less goodness, of course) is not. Amis has made a powerful career of depicting awful people and finding new ways to laugh at them. From Jim Dixon in his first novel to Harry Caldecote in

CONCLUSION

his latest, his "good" characters amuse us while demonstrating the virtues of common sense, emotional decency, and general morality.

Notes

1. Kingsley Amis, *I Like It Here* (New York: Harcourt, Brace, 1958) 112.

2. Dale Salwak, "An Interview with Kingsley Amis," *Contemporary Literature* 16 (1975): 5.

3. Kingsley Amis, *The Folks That Live on the Hill* (New York: Summit Books, 1990) 89.

BIBLIOGRAPHY

Books written or edited by Kingsley Amis

Bright November. London: Fortune Press, 1947. Poems.

Lucky Jim. London: Gollancz, 1954; Garden City, NY: Doubleday, 1954.

That Uncertain Feeling. London: Gollancz, 1955; New York: Harcourt, Brace, 1956.

A Case of Samples: Poems, 1945–1956. London: Gollancz, 1956; New York: Harcourt, Bracc, 1957.

Socialism and the Intellectuals. London: The Fabian Society, 1957.

I Like It Here. London: Gollancz, 1958; New York: Harcourt, Brace, 1958.

New Maps of Hell: A Survey of Science Fiction. New York: Harcourt, Brace, 1960; London: Gollancz, 1961.

Take a Girl Like You. London: Gollancz, 1960; New York: Harcourt, Brace & World, 1961.

My Enemy's Enemy. London: Gollancz, 1962; New York: Harcourt, Brace & World, 1963. Short Stories.

One Fat Englishman. London: Gollancz, 1963; New York: Harcourt, Brace & World, 1964.

The James Bond Dossier. London: Jonathan Cape, 1965; New York: New American Library, 1965.

The Egyptologists (with Robert Conquest). London: Jonathan Cape, 1965; New York: Random House, 1966.

The Anti-Death League. London: Gollancz, 1966; New York: Harcourt, Brace & World, 1966.

A Look Round the Estate: Poems 1957–1967. London: Jonathan Cape, 1967; New York: Harcourt, Brace & World, 1968.

Colonel Sun: A James Bond Adventure (under pseudonym Robert Markham). London: Jonathan Cape, 1968; New York: Harper & Row, 1968.

Lucky Jim's Politics. London: Conservative Political Centre, 1968.

BIBLIOGRAPHY

I Want It Now. London: Jonathan Cape, 1968; New York: Harcourt, Brace & World, 1969.

The Green Man. London: Jonathan Cape, 1969; New York: Harcourt, Brace & World, 1970.

What Became of Jane Austen? and Other Questions. London: Jonathan Cape, 1970; New York: Harcourt Brace Jovanovich, 1971.

Girl, 20. London: Jonathan Cape, 1971; New York: Harcourt Brace Jovanovich, 1972.

On Drink. London: Jonathan Cape, 1972; New York: Harcourt Brace Jovanovich, 1973.

The Riverside Villas Murder. London: Jonathan Cape, 1973; New York: Harcourt Brace Jovanovich, 1973.

Ending Up. London: Jonathan Cape, 1973; New York: Harcourt Brace Jovanovich, 1974.

Rudyard Kipling and His World. London: Thames and Hudson, 1975; New York: Scribners, 1976.

The Alteration. London: Jonathan Cape, 1976; New York: Viking Press, 1977.

Jake's Thing. London: Hutchinson, 1978; New York: Viking Press, 1979.

The New Oxford Book of Light Verse (editor). London and New York: Oxford University Press, 1978.

The Faber Popular Reciter (editor). London: Faber and Faber, 1978.

Russian Hide-and-Seek. London: Hutchinson, 1980.

Collected Short Stories. London: Hutchinson, 1980.

Collected Poems 1944–1979. London: Hutchinson, 1980; New York: Viking Press, 1981.

The Golden Age of Science Fiction (editor). London: Hutchinson, 1981.

Ever Day Drinking. London: Hutchinson, 1983.

BIBLIOGRAPHY

How's Your Glass? A Quizzical Look at Drinks and Drinking. London: Weidenfeld and Nicholson, 1984.

Stanley and the Women. London: Hutchinson, 1984; New York: Summit Books, 1985.

The Old Devils. London: Hutchinson, 1986; New York: Summit Books, 1987.

The Crime of the Century. London: J. M. Dent, 1987; New York: The Mysterious Press, 1990.

Difficulties with Girls. London: Hutchinson, 1988; New York: Summit Books, 1988.

The Folks That Live on the Hill. London: Hutchinson, 1990; New York: Summit Books, 1991.

The Amis Collection: Selected Non-Fiction 1954–1990. London: Hutchinson, 1990.

Memoirs. London: Hutchinson, 1991; New York: Summit Books, 1991.

Works about Kingsley Amis

Bibliographies

Gohn, J. B., *Kingsley Amis: A Checklist* (Kent, OH: Kent State University Press, 1976). Primary Bibliography.

Salwak, D. F., *Kingsley Amis: A Reference Guide* (Boston: G. K. Hall, 1978). Secondary Bibliography.

Books

Bradford, Richard. *Kingsley Amis.* London: Edward Arnold, 1989. Best at dispelling oversimplified judgments of Amis's moral positions. Covers works through *Stanley and the Women.*

Gardner, Philip. *Kingsley Amis.* Boston: Twayne, 1981. A serviceable overview of Amis's work up through *Jake's Thing* and *Collected Poems.* Well-written and sensible.

BIBLIOGRAPHY

McDermott, John. *Kingsley Amis: An English Moralist.* New York: St. Martin's, 1989. An excellent, thoughtful book covering works through *The Old Devils.* Good bibliography.

Salwak, Dale, ed. *Kingsley Amis in Life and Letters.* London: Macmillan, 1990. A strangely mixed collection of critical judgments, some quite sharp, and recollections by friends and acquaintances.

Articles and Sections of Books

Allen, Walter. *Tradition and Dream: The English and American Novel from the Twenties to Our Time.* London: Phoenix House, 1964. A survey, with some good commentary on Amis's "new kind of hero."

Ball, Patricia. "The Photographic Art." *Review of English Literature* 3 (April 1962): 50–58. Useful essay on Amis's poetry, relating it to Movement ideals.

Bergonzi, Bernard. *The Situation of the Novel.* Pittsburgh: University of Pittsburgh Press, 1970. Somewhat superficial, pigeonholing Amis too restrictively.

Bradbury, Malcolm. " 'No, Not Bloomsbury': The Comic Fiction of Kingsley Amis." *No, Not Bloomsbury.* New York: Columbia University Press, 1988. An excellent overview of Amis, properly assessing his strengths and weaknesses.

Brophy, Brigid. *Don't Never Forget.* New York: Holt, Rinehart, & Winston, 1966. Dismissive of Amis on ignorant grounds, including a puzzling inability to decide when Amis is satirizing his characters.

Brown, Craig. "Amis Buys His Round of Poison: Blokeish Bad Humour from the Lounge Bar." *Times Literary Supplement,* 8 March 1991: 9. Savage review of Amis's *Memoirs.*

Colville, Derek. "The Sane New World of Kingsley Amis." *Bucknell Review* 9 (March 1960): 46–57. Appreciates Amis but urges him to find more serious themes to write about.

BIBLIOGRAPHY

Conquest, Robert. "Christian Symbolism in *Lucky Jim.*" *Critical Quarterly* 7 (Spring 1965): 87–92. A spoof, pretending to see *Lucky Jim* as a religious book.

Farringdon, Jill. "When You Come Home Again to Wales: Kingsley Amis's *The Old Devils.*" *The Anglo-Welsh Review* 86 (1987): 87–91. A thoughtful review article written from a Welsh point of view.

Gibson, Walker. "You Mustn't Say Things Like That." *The Nation* 187 (November 29, 1958) 410–12. An appreciation of Amis's satire on dishonest language.

Gindin, James. "Kingsley Amis's Funny Novels." *Postwar British Fiction: New Accents and Attitudes.* Berkeley: University of California Press, 1962. Emphasis on comedy leads Gindin to overlook moral issues.

————. "The Reassertion of the Personal." *Texas Quarterly* 1 (Winter 1958): 126–34. Tries to "place" Amis with Huxley, Murdoch, Wilson, and other mid-century British writers.

————. "Well Beyond Laughter: Directions from Fifties' Comic Fiction." *Studies in the Novel* 3 (Winter 1971): 357–64. Overgeneralizes about Amis, failing to notice new directions in the fiction.

Green, Martin. "British Comedy & The British Sense of Humour: Shaw, Waugh, and Amis." *Texas Quarterly* 4 (Autumn 1961): 217–27. Green's acuteness on Amis is compromised by his insistence on connecting him with Lawrence.

————. "British Decency." *The Kenyon Review* 21 (Autumn 1959): 505–32. Scotches the idea that Amis's characters are "would-be gentlemen"; arrays him with Orwell, Lawrence, Leavis.

Hamilton, Kenneth. "Kingsley Amis, Moralist." *Dalhousie Review* 44 (1964): 339–47. General survey, pointing to serious themes.

Hewison, Robert. *In Anger: British Culture in the Cold War 1945–60.* New York: Oxford University Press, 1981. Solid on political background and on the Movement.

BIBLIOGRAPHY

Hilty, Peter. "Kingsley Amis and Mid-Century Humor." *Discourse* 3 (January 1960): 26–45. An unfortunate early article embarrassingly condescending to Amis.

Hopkins, Robert H. "The Satire of Kingsley Amis's *I Like It Here*." *Critique* 8 (Spring/Summer 1966): 62–70. Argues that the book is a satire on Leavis's *The Great Tradition*.

Hurrell, John D. "Class and Conscience in John Braine and Kingsley Amis." *Critique* 2 (1958–59): 39–53. Strong on moral issues of *Lucky Jim*.

Hutchings, W. "Kingsley Amis's Counterfeit World." *Critical Quarterly* 19 (Summer 1977): 71–77. Unusual in its serious attention to *The Alteration*.

Jones, D. A. N. "Kingsley Amis." *Grand Street* 4 (Spring 1985): 206–14. Good on the controversy about *Stanley and the Women*.

Kelly, Edward. "Satire and Word Games in Amis's *Englishman*." *Satire Newsletter* 9 (Spring 1972): 132–38. An unusual look at *One Fat Englishman* concentrating on wordplay and Micheldene's fastidiousness about language.

Lee, Hermione. "Kingsley and the Women." *The New Republic* 201 (July 31, 1989): 39–40. A review of *Difficulties with Girls* containing unfair but strongly felt generalizations about late Amis and misogyny.

Lodge, David. "The Modern, the Contemporary, and the Importance of Being Amis," *Language of Fiction*. New York: Columbia University Press, 1966. One of the most important essays on Amis; Lodge relates Amis well to modernist writing, and comments perceptively on his novels through *Take a Girl Like You*.

————. *Write On: Occasional Essays '65–'85*. London: Secker & Warburg, 1986. Interesting comments on Amis's liberating role for young writers in the 1950s and on the Movement.

BIBLIOGRAPHY

McCabe, Bernard. "Looking for the Simple Life: Kingsley Amis's *The Anti-Death League* (1966)." *Old Lines, New Forces: Essays on the Contemporary British Novel, 1960–1970*. Ed. Robert K. Morris. Rutherford: Fairleigh Dickinson University Press, 1976, 67–80. Sees the book as anti-God satire.

McDermott, John. "Kingsley and the Women." *Critical Quarterly* 27 (Autumn 1985): 65–71. Defends Amis against accusations of misogyny.

Macleod, Norman. "A Trip to Greeneland: The Plagiarizing Narrator of Kingsley Amis's *I Like It Here*." *Studies in the Novel* 17 (Summer 1985): 203–17. An overly subtle argument for Amis's ironic self-self-parody based on the hidden "plagiarisms" of Graham Greene by the narrator.

———. "*This Familiar Regressive Series:* Aspects of Style in the Novels of Kingsley Amis." *Edinburgh Studies in English and Scots*. Ed. A. J. Aitken, et. al. London: Longman, 1971. Careful and interesting examination of Amis's language, especially grammatical forms which mimic self-consciousness and self-correction.

O'Connor, William Van. *The New University Wits and the End of Modernism*. Carbondale: Southern Illinois University Press, 1963. Discusses Amis, Wain, Larkin, Murdoch, from "university wits" point of view rather than more familiar "angry" one.

———. "Two Types of 'Heroes' in Post-War British Fiction." *PMLA* 77 (March 1962): 168–74. Good definition of the new type of protagonist represented by Jim Dixon.

Orel, Harold. "The Decline and Fall of a Comic Novelist: Kingsley Amis." *Kansas Quarterly* 1 (Summer 1969): 17–22. Biting commentary, attempting to correlate Amis's "decline" with his commercial success.

BIBLIOGRAPHY

Paul, Leslie. "The Angry Young Men Revisited." *The Kenyon Review* 27 (Spring 1965). The coiner of the "angry young man" term is disappointed with the direction the writers took after the mid-1950s.

Parker, R. B. "Farce and Society: The Range of Kingsley Amis." *Wisconsin Studies in Contemporary Literature* 2 (Fall 1961): 27–38. Disappointed that Amis's work is not more socially radical.

Pazereskis, John. "Kingsley Amis—The Dark Side." *Studies in Contemporary Satire* 4 (1977): 28–33. A bit overwrought but comments on too-often overlooked *Green Man* and *Anti-Death League*.

Rabinovitz, Rubin. *The Reaction Against Experiment in the English Novel, 1950–1960*. New York: Columbia University Press, 1967. Ranks Amis among older authors C. P. Snow and Angus Wilson as reactionaries; aligns Jim's "philistinism" with the author.

Roberts, G. O. "Love and Death in an English Novel: *The Anti-Death League* Investigated." *A Festschrift for Edgar Ronald Seary*, ed. A. A. Macdonald et. al. St. John's: Memorial University of Newfoundland, 1975, 200–14. Appreciative treatment of this book.

Scott, J. D. "Britain's Angry Young Men." *The Saturday Review* 40 (July 27, 1957): 8–11. Includes a "gallery of Lucky Jims"—the usual ones: John Osborne, John Braine, John Wain, along with Amis.

Teachout, Terry. "A Touch of Class." *The New Criterion* 7 (November 1988): 8–17. An appreciative overview, not very reliable on details.

Voorhees, Richard J. "Kingsley Amis: Three Hurrahs and a Reservation." *Queens Quarterly* 74 (Spring 1972): 38–46. An appreciation that compares Amis to Fielding in both comedy and moral judgment.

BIBLIOGRAPHY

Watson, George. "The Coronation of Realism." *Georgia Review* 41 (Spring 1987): 5–16. The coronation is that of Elizabeth II, placing Amis in history; Watson says Amis's type of novel assumes that language is referential.

Wilmes, D. R. "When the Curse Begins to Hurt: Kingsley Amis and Satiric Confrontation." *Studies in Contemporary Satire* 5 (1978): 9–21. A bit carried away with Amis's purported satiric mission against ills of the world.

Wilson, Edmund. *The Bit Between My Teeth: A Literary Chronicle of 1950–1965*. New York: Farrar, Straus and Giroux, 1965. Perceptive comments on the early books, especially *That Uncertain Feeling*.

Wilson, Keith. "Jim, Jake and the Years Between: The Will to Stasis in the Contemporary British Novel." *Ariel* 13 (January 1982): 55–69. Interestingly relates *Jake's Thing* to seventies novels by Burgess, Drabble, Fowles, and Golding, all of them gloomy "condition of England" books.

Interviews and Profiles

Barber, Michael. "The Art of Fiction LIX: Kingsley Amis." *Paris Review* 64 (1975): 39–72. A very good, far-ranging interview.

Hennessy, Val. *A Little Light Friction*. London: Futura Publications, 1989: 202–207. Reports on an unsuccessful interview, just after publication of *Stanley and the Women*.

Firchow, Peter, ed. *The Writer's Place: Interviews on the Literary Situation in Contemporary Britain*. Minneapolis: University of Minnesota Press, 1974, 15–38. Better on the literary *situation* than on Amis's books.

James, Clive. "Profile 4: Kingsley Amis." *The New Review* 1 (July 1974): 21–28. Good interview; perceptive additional comments by James.

BIBLIOGRAPHY

Salwak, Dale. "An Interview With Kingsley Amis." *Contemporary Literature* 16 (Winter 1975): 1–18. Good comments by Amis, including how he got started and his ideas for books.

———— . "Kingsley Amis: Mimic and Moralist." *Interviews with Britain's Angry Young Men*. San Bernardino, CA: Borgo Press, 1984. Reprints the 1975 interview and extends it with a later interview.

Index

187

188

INDEX

INDEX

INDEX

INDEX

INDEX